The Quotable Golfer

The Quotable Golfer

EDITED BY
ROBERT McCORD

Main Street
A division of Sterling Publishing Co., Inc.
New York

Library of Congress Cataloging-in-Publication Data available

10 9 8 7 6 5 4 3 2 1

Published by Main Street, a division of Sterling Publishing Co., Inc.
387 Park Avenue South, New York, NY 10016

Introduction and order copyright © 2000 by Robert McCord
Revised editon copyright © 2004 by Sterling Publishing
Distributed in Canada by Sterling Publishing
c/o Canadian Manda Group, One Atlantic Avenue, Suite 105
Toronto, Ontario, Canada M6K 3E7
Distributed in Great Britain by Chrysalis Books Group PLC
The Chrysalis Building, Bramley Road, London W10 6SP, England
Distributed in Australia by Capricorn Link (Australia) Pty. Ltd.
P.O. Box 704, Windsor, NSW 2756, Australia

Sterling ISBN   1-4027-1426-2

To Belinda,

My Sweet Potato

Contents

Acknowledgements

Many thanks to Nick Lyons, founder of Lyons Press and a skilled writer, teacher, and publishing gentleman who asked me to do this book and who gently, but tenaciously pushed it through to completion. Also thanks to Jonathan McCullough and the rest of the team at Lyons Press. And finally, thanks to all of those golfers, golf writers, and other players in the golf world who contributed, directly or indirectly to the contents of this book.

All shanks, hooks, slices and chili dips contained herein are my responsibility.

Introduction

Golf is almost Shakespearean in its elegant commingling of comedy, absurdity, heroism and tragedy acted out by a panoply of characters ranging from weekend duffers, such as myself, to those in the pantheon of the game, such as Tom Morris, Joyce Wethered, Bobby Jones, Babe Zaharias, Walter Hagen, Ben Hogan, Mickey Wright, Arnold Palmer, Nancy Lopez, Jack Nicklaus and all the rest. Often golf appears to be a Sisyphean exercise—we always seem to be pushing a very large boulder up a hill while venturing along the course. But any anguish and frustration are alleviated by that occasional perfect shot, the good company of other golfers, and the often beautiful and challenging courses where we match wits with the fates.

The Quotable Golfer is a collection of observations on the game from the great, near great and not too great, who, in their own ways, contribute to its lore and richness. In aggregate, the compiling of these quotes is an attempt to illustrate the richness of the golf experience and its limitless possibilities and limitations—that endless roller coaster we all ride whenever we pick up a club.

I hope that you find some enjoyment among these pages. The pleasure was mine in reading the material to get to this point. But finally I had to stop. Now it's your turn to play.

—Robert McCord
New York City
January, 2000

The Quotable Golfer

1

Golf Defined

Golf: A game probably evolved from Dutch antecedents, first recorded in Scotland in the 15th century, and played under codified rules since the middle of the 18th century; now consisting of hitting a golf ball, using an array of golf clubs, by successive strokes into each of nine or eighteen holes on a golf course.

—FROM *THE RULES OF GOLF*, published by the Royal and Ancient Golf Club in St. Andrews, Scotland, and the United States Golf Association, Far Hills, New Jersey

... we saw elderly citizens playing at the Old Scots game of golf, which is a kind of gigantic variety of billiards.

—PETER MORRIS, from *Peter's Letters to His Kinsfolk* (1819)

No one will ever have golf under his thumb. No round ever will be so good it could not have been better. Perhaps this is why golf is the greatest of games. You are not playing a human adversary; you are playing a game. You are playing old man par.

—BOBBY JONES, the greatest amateur golfer of all time.

Golf is just one thing to me—the pure pleasure of the golf swing.

—MICKEY WRIGHT, winner of 82 LPGA tournaments

———•••———

I think at that time I really fell in love with the game. I'd always loved golf, but now it was a new type of love that I could have.

—TOM WATSON, after his one-shot win over Jack Nicklaus in the 1977 British Open

The thing that sets golf apart from the other sports is that it takes self-confidence, an ability to rely totally on yourself. When I'm through, I'll really miss kicking myself to get it done. I can live without playing the Masters. But the really satisfying time is the three weeks leading up to the Masters when I'm preparing for it.

—JACK NICKLAUS, winner of six Masters (1963, 1965, 1966, 1972, 1975, 1986)

Golf increases the blood pressure, ruins the disposition, spoils the digestion, induces neurasthenia, hurts the eyes, calluses the hands, ties knots in the nervous system, debauches the morals, drives men to drink or homicide, breaks up the family, turns the ductless glands into internal warts, corrodes the pneumogastric nerve, breaks off the edges of the vertebrae, induces spinal meningitis and progressive mendacity, and starts angina pectoris.

—DR. A. S. LAMB, McGill University

The golfer has more enemies that any other athlete. He has fourteen clubs in his bag, all of them different; 18 holes to play, all of them different, every week; and all around him is sand, trees, grass, water, wind and 143 other players. In addition, the game is 50 percent mental, so his biggest enemy is himself.

—DAN JENKINS, golf writer, describing golf on the PGA Tour

Golf is a good walk spoiled.

—MARK TWAIN

I am a slave to golf.

—ENID WILSON, winner of the 1925 British Girls' title

Rock-a-bye, baby—til father comes home;
Father's off golfing and mother's alone;
He phoned me this morning—he wanted his cleek;
Perhaps he'll be home again, sometime next week.

—"MOTHER GOOSE ON THE LINKS," 1909

Golf is about how well you accept, respond to, and score with your misses much more so than it is a game of your perfect shots.

—DR. BOB ROTELLA, sports psychologist and consultant to golfers in 1997

I simply wanted to do nothing. . . . My nothing meant simply to play golf . . . This may seem incredible to those who have never fallen hopelessly in love with the game; but I can see the charm and temptation even now, for golf or any other pastime can be much more than a mere hitting of the ball; it can be, however poor a one, a life to be lived. To dwell near a good course and work hard at the game; to go away whenever the spirit moved one north, south, east, or west, to some paradise by the seas with a pleasant companion or two; to stay as long as one liked, and then move to another course and another set of friends . . . even to think of it is still to feel faintly the old desire.

—BERNARD DARWIN, member of the 1922 British Walker Cup team, and author of several golf books, recalling why he gave up the practice of law to play and write about golf

Rail-splitting produced an immortal president in Lincoln, but golf hasn't produced even a good A1 Congressman.

—WILL ROGERS, American humorist

Golf courses are the best place to observe ministers, but none of them are above cheating a bit.

—JOHN D. ROCKEFELLER, oil billionaire and avid golfer

Golf is an awkward set of bodily contortions designed to produce a graceful result.

—TOMMY ARMOUR, golf instructor and winner of the U.S. Open (1927), PGA (1930) and British Open (1931)

When I was a schoolgirl my idea of good golf was a good drive. What happens afterwards did not matter. I was perfectly content to suffer the most grievous trouble if I smacked the ball 200 yards off the tee. Fortunately, I revised my ideas fairly quickly and settled down to practising the various kinds of approach play, determined to master all of them.

—PAMELA BARTON, winner of both the British Ladies' and U.S. Women's Amateurs in 1936

Golf is twenty percent mechanics and technique. The other eighty percent is philosophy, humor, tragedy, romance, melodrama, companionship, camaraderie, cussedness and conversation.

—GRANTLAND RICE, noted American sports writer and avid golfer until his death in 1954 at age 74

Playing golf is like eating. It's something which has to come naturally.

—SAM SNEAD, winner of a record 81 official PGA Tour events

Pain and suffering are inevitable in our lives, but misery is an option.

> —CHIP BECK, winner of over $5 million on the PGA Tour, on the vicissitudes of golf

I am not talking about ladies' golf because strictly speaking, there is no such thing as ladies' golf—only good or bad golf played by the member of either sex.

> —JOYNCE WETHERED, winner of five consecutive English Ladies' titles (1920–1924) including 33 matches in succession

Middle age occurs when you are too young to take up golf and too old to rush up to the net.

—FRANKLIN PIERCE ADAMS

—◦•⊙•◦—

Why do I enjoy golf after 31 years, going out there and doing the things that are necessary to be competitive—having to practice, having to work, having to dedicate yourself? I guess it comes down to the competition. My personality is such that I'm not going to play if I'm not competitive.

—RAYMOND FLOYD, in a *Golf Digest* interview in 1994

Golf is a game in which you claim the privileges of age and retain the playthings of childhood.

—SAMUEL JOHNSON

———

I thought everybody was named Labron and Byron, talked with a Texas accent, and said, "Nice shot, padnah."

—AMY ALCOTT, winner of over $3 million on the LPGA tour on, on how television influenced her to chose golf over tennis at age 9

I may know I am better than an 18, but the computer absorbs my scores year after year and continues to tell me that is what I am. Therein lies the tragedy of golf. We know what we should be, but there is always some number telling us what it is. . . .

—PETER ANDREWS, golf writer, on the tragedy of golf numbers

Golf is like acting in that both require concentration and relaxation at the same time. In acting, you can't push emotion. You have to let it rise from you naturally. Same thing in golf. You have to have a plan and a focus; but then you need to just let it happen and enjoy the smooth movement of the swing.

—JANE SEYMOUR, actress and high handicapper

No sport is so underrated in terms of dedication needed and skill required. It's you against everyone, and yet you alone against the course. It is the most individual of all sports, and no amount of camaraderie prior to a match can change the fact that you're in it alone. Your coach must stand silent on the sidelines; your teammates are scattered across one hundred acres of playing field. There's no one to cover up for a hooked drive, no one to tap in a missed putt. No scoreboard, no half time rally.

—BARBARA BALDWIN, writer and mother observing her teenage son playing competitive golf

There is a basic fascination with golf unlike other games. No ordinary person could go one round with the heavyweight boxing champion, expect to hit a Nolan Ryan fastball, throw a football like Joe Montana, or leap from the free-throw line for a reverse overhead dunk like Michael Jordan. But a golfer may at any time hit that one spectacular shot just as well as Ben Hogan, Arnold Palmer, or Greg Norman. Just the chance to do that is what keeps bringing them back.

—PETE DYE, golf architect, designer of PGA West, Crooked Stick, the Kiawah Ocean Course and other challenging golf courses

Golf is a game in which you try to put a small ball in a small hole with implements singularly unsuited to the purpose.

—WINSTON CHURCHILL

Golf is not, on the whole, a game for realists. By its exactitudes of measurement, it invites the attention of perfectionists.

—HEYWOOD HALE BROUN, American sportswriter

Playing Golf is not hot work. Cutting sugar cane for a dollar a day—that's hot work. Hotter than my first wrist watch.

—CHI-CHI RODRIGUEZ, a native of Bayamón, Puerto Rico, and winner of over $6 million of the Senior PGA Tour

Every shot in golf should be played as a shot at some clearly defined target. All players realize this when they are playing a shot to the green. A narrow opening between bunkers, or the pin itself, may be the target. But what many of them forget is the shot off the tee should also be aimed at the target down the fairway.

—CRAIG WOOD, winner of the Masters and U.S. Open in 1921

The pond'rous club upon the ball
  Descends
Involved in dust th' exulting orb
  Ascends

> —THOMAS MATHISON, in *The Goff*, the first golf book ever
> written, in 1743

———————

But there is a difference between playing well and
hitting the ball well. Hitting the ball well is about
thirty percent of it. The rest is being comfortable
with the different situations on the course.

> —MICKEY WRIGHT, winner of a single season record 13
> LPGA Tour victories in 1963

The golfer, though, stands alone. He starts and finishes the deed; every shot he plays is a one-on-one confrontation with his own nervous system, power of concentration, ego. He can blame no one for failure, can take full credit for success. Unlike any other game player, the golfer can go virtually alone into the breach and have himself a tilt. It is just he and the golf course, and the latter essentially passive. The golfer is Don Quixote attacking a windmill, a windmill that is literally, and by the way, figuratively, himself.

—AL BARKOW, from *Golf's Golden Grind: a History of the Tour* (1974)

That's the hard thing, the time it takes to keep yourself prepared. That I still have the discipline and the desire to get out there day after day, beat balls and putt and chip, do my hour of stretching and exercise. I really don't understand why I keep doing that. I guess we could go ask Arnold. I guess it is something that is there in you and never goes away.

—RAYMOND FLOYD, in a *Golf Digest* interview in 1994

A round of golf partakes of the journey, and the journey is one of the central myths and signs of Western man . . . if it is a journey, it is also a round: it always leads back to the place where you started from . . . golf is always a trip back to the first tee, the more you play the more you realize you are staying where you are. By playing golf you reenact that secret of the journey. You may even get to enjoy it.

—Shivas Irons, from *Golf in the Kingdom* by Michael Murphy (1972)

2

Beginnings

They say golf came easy to me because I was a good athlete, but there's not any girl on the LPGA Tour who worked near as hard as I did in golf. It is the toughest game I ever tackled.

> —BABE ZAHARIAS, winner of 17 consecutive amateur tournaments in 1946 and 1947 and a member of the LPGA Hall of Fame

———•·•·•———

My family was so poor they couldn't afford kids. The lady next door had me.

> —LEE TREVINO

I do not recall the first time I hit a golf ball, or hit at one; and as I recall it the game did not make much of an impression on me, except that I used to get mad enough to dance in the road when a wild shot went under a little bridge covered with briers across the ditch which was on the second hole. I liked baseball much better, and played golf, or what we called golf, because of a dearth of boys in the neighborhood with whom to play baseball.

—BOBBY JONES

The hardest thing was being young and coming onto the tour right out of high school and a very close home environment. I think the thing I missed most was my mother's homemade soup.

—AMY ALCOTT, recalling her early days on the LPGA Tour

When I was three . . . my father put my hands in his and placed them around the shaft of a cut-down women's golf club. He showed me the classic overlap, or Vardon grip—the proper grip for a good golf swing he said—and told me to hit the golf ball . . . "Hit it hard boy. Go find it and hit it again."

—ARNOLD PALMER, from *A Golfer's Life,* with James Dodson (1999)

I started to play golf when I was three. Alice was nine. Six years later, dad loaded the family belongings into a Model-A Ford pickup and moved all of us west (from South Dakota) to California where the plan was for Alice and me to play year-round on real grass courses. We lived in a tiny house they'd bought in Lakewood City so Alice and I could play at a Long Beach public course. I believe there was $8 left in the family bank account when we finally got settled.

—MARLENE BAUER HAGGE, who, at age 18 was the youngest player to win an LPGA event, the 1952 Sarasota Open

I feel sorry for rich kids now. I really do. Because they're never going to have the opportunity I had. Because I knew tough things, and I had a tough day all my life and can handle tough things. They can't. And every day that I progressed was a joy to me and I recognized it every day. I don't think I could have done it if I hadn't had the tough days to begin with.

—BEN HOGAN in *Hogan* by Curt Sampson (1998)

The most important advice I'd give any woman just starting to play is: get the fundamentals correct. It's a bad mistake simply to pick up a club and start swinging. If you can afford them, lessons from a competent pro will be worth their weight in birdies; if money is a consideration, join a group to take lessons.

—LOUISE SUGGS, member of the LPGA Hall of Fame

If you're going to be a victim of the first few holes, you don't have a prayer. You're like a puppet. You let the first few holes jerk your strings and tell you how you're going to feel and how you're going to think.

—DR. BOB ROTELLA, noted sports psychologist (1999)

I had a natural golf swing, they said. With proper instruction, I could hit a golf ball as far, if not farther, than any of the women golfers. Dad was elated. As I came off the course after that round, my destiny was settled. I would become a golfer.

—GLENNA COLLETT, winner of a record six U.S. Women's Amateurs, after playing a first round of golf with her father

. . . I fancy that having at first played the game almost entirely by the light of nature he [Gene Sarazen] took to thinking about it. That is a thing that has almost got happen to any good young golfer at some time, and occasionally the young golfer is never so good again afterwards; the first "careless rapture" of hitting, the splendid confidence are never satisfactorily replaced.

—BERNARD DARWIN, writer for *The London Times* and *Country Life* from 1907 to 1953

I can only thank Davis Love III for turning me on to golf and showing me it isn't a sissy game.

—MICHAEL JORDAN, former NBA superstar, who first took up golf in college

I started golf at 8. Dad had an auto-body repair shop. He and mom sacrificed all the time. Every extra cent was used to get me into amateur tournaments. They gave up things to make sure I had clothes that looked nice. They would go without, so I could have three new balls or new socks. My wonderful parents gave me the opportunity to compete with the best and get the experience I needed to be successful.

—NANCY LOPEZ, who won the New Mexico Women's Amateur at age 12

Just offer the opportunity. Put the clubs in the corner and give them access to a place to play. That might mean driving them to a course, or just buying them a bicycle. Anything more than that and you can run the risk of turning off your children to a game they could enjoy their whole life...

—NICK PRICE, on how to be a golfing father

Nobody wants to work for anything. We have a deal for juniors at my club. You caddie, you get free golf. Nobody comes. They'd rather drive their BMWs. You pass baseball fields, nobody is there. They'd rather play Nintendo. When I earned a golf scholarship you had to shoot in the 70s. Now they are giving them to kids who shoot 80.

—JULIE INKSTER, LPGA Hall of Famer and winner of three straight U.S. Women's Amateurs (1980–82)

A kid grows up a lot faster on the golf course; golf teaches you how to behave. You start playing with older people so that a kid who plays golf is different from a lot of athletes in other sports because he hasn't had his own way. He hasn't been spoiled.

—JACK NICKLAUS, U.S. Amateur Champion in 1959 and 1961

Fight! Fight! Fight! Why is that always preached to a young golfer? After all, if you hold the majority of the good cards, you can stand a fine chance of beating Cuthbertson at bridge. My theory is this: if you perfect your golf shots, your opponent will need more than an unfriendly attitude to defeat you.

—VIRGINIA VAN WIE, a leading American amateur golfer (1934)

There is simply no point at which the notion of pressure becomes intimidating. For Tiger, there cannot be pressure because the worst thing that can happen to him is nothing. His parents still love him and his life will go on as he envisions . . . it is a gift from his parents.

>—CHUCK HOGAN, golf instructor, on Tiger Woods, the youngest golfer to win the U.S. Amateur Championship, at age 18 in 1994

Fine. I've frozen enough of my life. Why should you have to?

>—BOBO SHEEHAN to his daughter, Patty, when she told him, at age 13, she wanted to give up a promising competitive skiing career to play golf

If beginners and club golfers as a whole were to absorb and fully understand four or five basic principles, they would get themselves into a position from which they could hit the ball consistently. I believe the basic principles of the golf swing are rhythm, stance, grip, the takeaway from the ball and the head. Of these, one of the most important is rhythm, and every player must learn for himself what rhythm means to him.

—GEORGE WILL, writer, in "Advice for Men and Women Players"

I learned by copying. My father used to take Roger and me to watch golf when we were youngsters, and I tried to copy the good players' rhythm. Then, when I began playing fairly well, I played a lot with Roger and his friends from Oxford.

—JOYCE WETHERED, the world's leading woman golfer in the 1920s and 1930s

Whenever I had gone for several days without seeing her, I would refresh my spirit by repeating to myself: "We don't ever see you playing golf," with the nasal intonation in which she uttered the words, point blank, without moving a muscle in her face. And I thought that there could be no one in the world as desirable.

—MARCEL PROUST, in "Within a Budding Grove" from *On First Meeting Albertine*

I don't know enough to take you where you need to be.

—HARDY LOUDERMILK, golf instructor, to LPGA Hall of Famer, Kathy Whitworth, when she was 17

I needed to be pushed. As a youngster I didn't recognize my true ability or talents. And, yes, I had a little bit of rebellion in me. I wanted to be with the gang. Sure, I said I was going to the golf course, but when I got my driver's license, man, as soon as I got out of sight, I took the next left.

—PAT BRADLEY, who was inducted into the LPGA Hall of Fame in 1991

Between 10 and 13, you play 54 holes a day with your friends and golf pros give you lessons for free. Then, when you're 16, you go on the Teen Tour. If you make the national boys' team, you travel on your summer vacation playing tournaments. It's very structured, but it isn't like American Little League. It isn't for parents, it's for you.

—JESPER PARNEVIK, describing the development of Swedish golfers

I was a good student. Phi Beta Kappa. I studied a lot, and that helped my concentration. Maybe it helps to have a very controlled logical sort of mind to play golf. I studied physics in college, and my father was an engineer. Maybe there was something to that. Of course you also have to play a lot when you are young. You have to pay your dues. . . .

—BETSY RAWLS, member of the LPGA Hall of Fame, and fourth in all-time wins with 55, behind Kathy Whitworth, Mickey Wright and Patty Berg

Why do I love kids so much? Because I never was a kid myself. I was too poor to be a child, so I never really had a childhood. The biggest present I ever got was a marble.

—CHI-CHI RODRIGUEZ, who won his first PGA Tour event in 1963 at age 27

3

Obstacles

Those who the gods seek to destroy first, learn how to play golf.

—Leslie Nielsen in the video, *Bad Golf My Way*

<hr />

The world's No.1 tennis player spends 90 percent of his time winning, while the world's No.1 golfer spends 90 percent of his time losing. Golfers are great losers.

—David Feherty, journeyman professional

One of the objects in placing hazards is to give the players as much pleasurable excitement as possible.

—ALISTER MACKENZIE, golf course architect, from his classic *Golf Architecture*

———

I am among those who firmly believe that a round of golf should not take more than 3½ hours, four at most. Anything longer than that is not a round of golf, it's life in Albania.

—DAN JENKINS, golf writer, on slow play

Golf was a game supported by rich men who did the hiring and firing, the pros were servants.

> —AL BARKOW, writing about the lowly status of professionals in the early days of golf

———

Before Hagen broke down the walls of prejudice, a professional golfer had no standing whatever.

> —GENE SARAZEN in Herbert Warren Wind's, *The Complete Golfer* (1950)

No dogs or women.

—SIGN AT THE ENTRANCE TO A GOLF CLUB

The golf links lie so near the mill
   That almost every day
The laboring children can look out
   And watch the men at play.

—SARAH N. CLEGHORN, on golf and child labor in 1915

How do they learn to play? Courses are so busy and many of them are restrictive for kids. I worry about this.

—BILL OGDEN, former club professional, North Shore Country Club

———————

Sneaky cheaters are people who suffer from that old devil "low self-esteem" and are lured to cheat at golf in the same way they might drift into alcoholism. They are looking for ways to justify the internal image. "I may not be much of a man," they say, "but I can sure as hell win this golf match." They don't do anything big. Just a nudge here and there to give themselves an edge. They would be devastated if they ever were caught....

—PETER ANDREWS, golf writer and commentator in an article "Cheaters Bold and Sneaky" in *Golf Digest*

The only area where I have ever experienced discrimination is athletics. Growing up, I couldn't play little league baseball or be on the high school golf team simply because I was a girl. But that's changing. My alma mater, Furman University, now has five full golf scholarships for women. There weren't any when I went there. . . .

> —BETSY KING, winner of the U.S. Women's Open in 1989 and 1990

Why do men have the right to feel superior? I think women are far superior to men, or at any rate, we're all equal. I don't see why I can't have the same rights as a man.

> —MARY ANDERSON, Chair of the Ladies' Golf Union, reacting to discriminatory practices against lady golfers in England in 1991

It's pretty much a miracle that a bullet can go through your neck and not hit anything vital.

> —KIM WILLIAMS, after being accidentally shot in the neck by a stray bullet from a target shooter at the Youngstown-Warren LPGA Classic in 1994

Some players would complain if the were playing on Dolly Parton's bedspread.

> —JIMMY DEMARET, winner of 31 career PGA events

. . . Don't get into the habit of using "winter rules." If you do, you'll never learn to be a decent golfer. "Winter rules" are generally an amusing delusion. They aid neither in the development of the turf nor of the player.

—TOMMY ARMOUR, in *How to Play Your Best Golf All the Time* (1961)

———

When facing a hazard, focus your attention sharply on your target, not the hazard.

—DR. BOB ROTELLA, sports psychologist

When a ball lies on clothes, or within one club length of a washing tub, the clothes may be drawn from under the ball and the tub removed.

—AN 1851 RULE, issued by the Royal & Ancient for hazards caused by townswomen who washed their clothes in the Swilcan Burn, the water hazard that now cuts the first and eighteenth fairways on the Old Course

A good player prays for wind every day, but not too earnestly.

—JOHN L. LOW, in *Concerning Golf* (1903)

Bobby Jones told me he used to run back to Stewart Maiden during those seven lean years of his career for lessons. He said that when he learned to be able to correct himself on the golf course, control his own game and do it himself, that's when he became a good player. Now if you are going to continue to rely on somebody every time, you never end up doing it yourself.

—JACK NICKLAUS, in *Golf Digest* (1991)

Herman, would you check on my clubs?

—BEN HOGAN, to fellow PGA pro Herman Keiser from his hospital bed, shortly after Hogan was almost killed in an automobile accident in 1949

I couldn't figure it out. My marriage was fine, my kids were healthy, and everything was good. But I wasn't happy with me. So I went on a low-fat diet and started exercising. I wasn't feeling competitive the previous year; I was just playing golf and that's all.

—NANCY LOPEZ, member of the LPGA Hall of Fame, in 1997

Christ, most people'd be drunk for two days on what I have before dinner.

—JOHN DALY, winner of the PGA Championship and British Open, on his battle with alcoholism

I can't go out and party as much as I want. I have to behave. It's a big change for me and I'm doing it little by little.

—HELEN ALFREDSSON, LPGA Tour player

I expect to hit at least five bad shots.

—WALTER HAGEN, on how he expects obstacles

Ma God! It's like playing up a spout.

—JAMIE ANDERSON, winner of three consecutive British Opens (1877–1899), after hitting five balls out of bounds on the old first hole at Hoylake

The biggest problem we have in golf is course conditions.

> —Seve Ballesteros, on the poor condition of European Tour courses

I don't like the idea of golf widows. I was raised to believe I could do anything a man can do.

> —Jane Seymour, actress and 34 handicapper

Finally I'm vindicated. I'm certainly one of the most talented athletes ever to come out of the Chicago area, and I've been largely unappreciated. People like George Halas and the Wrigley family and Ditka have kept me down all these years, but at least I'm able to claim the glory that is rightly mine . . . I am now recognized as a true athletic hero.

> —BILL MURRAY, comedian, after hitting a flop wedge to within four feet of the pin on the 18th to defeat Michael Jordan and D. A. Weibring in a charity event in Chicago

I'll be playing center for the Bulls before Michael plays on the Tour.

> —PETER JACOBSEN, veteran PGA Tour player, assessing Michael Jordan's chances of joining the Tour

He's made one of the greatest attempts to play of any athlete I've seen.

> —PAYNE STEWART, on fellow PGA pro Paul Azinger's fight against cancer in 1994

I'm so tired of getting operated on. I'd rather die almost than have another operation, but I may not have a choice.

> —JOHNNY MILLER, former PGA Tour player and NBC-TV golf commentator

I had a good chance to get in the Masters if I finished good. And I was going good. Suddenly I was intercepted by five white men who started following me around the course. They threw their beer cans at me and called me "nigger" and other names. This went on for several holes and the men were finally arrested, but, after I lost a lot of strokes and finished far down the list.

—CHARLIE SIFFORD, African-American golfer, on his experience in the 1959 Greensboro Open

Involving minorities in the game of golf has financial, political and social implications. But the bottom line is simple: the more people who play the game, the fewer problems we'll have in the world. Because the game itself teaches people so much about themselves and others.

> —EARL WOODS, father of Eldrick "Tiger" Woods, winner of three U.S. Junior Boys and three U.S. Amateur Championships

I don't know if you're ever finished trying to improve. As soon as you feel like you are finished, then I guess you are finished, because you've already put a limit on your ability and what you can attain. I don't think that's right.

> —TIGER WOODS, after winning his 8th tournament in 1999, the World Golf Championship in Sotogrande, Spain

4

Practice

Never try a shot you haven't practiced.

—HARVEY PENICK, golf instructor and author of *Harvey Penick's Little Red Book*

———◆•◆•◆———

I've never had a coach in my life. When I find one who can beat me, then I'll listen.

—LEE TREVINO, winner of 27 PGA Tour events

The more I practice the luckier I get.

—GARY PLAYER, thirteen-time winner of the South
Africa Open

If you take only one golf lesson in your life, let it
deal only with grip, stance, alignment, ball position
and developing a routine that enables you to mentally and physically set up every time.

—DR. BOB ROTELLA, sports psychologist, in 1997

Very few times in my life I laid off two to three days. It seemed like it took me a month to three months to get back those three days when I took a rest. It's a tough situation. I had to practice all the time.

—BEN HOGAN, winner of four U.S. Opens

———◆•••◆———

When the old question "What is the most important part of the game?" is thrown at me, I don't have to think twice. I answer, "the grip." Without that basic, anyone's form is bound to be erratic. From the grip we build to the stance and from the stance we graduate to the heart of the game itself, the swing. These are the imperatives. Without them, one can't achieve the status of a duffer; with them one has a game. The rest is merely refinement.

—LOUISE SUGGS, charter member of the LPGA Hall of Fame

Don't play too much golf if you want to get on in the game. Three rounds a day are too much for any man, and if he makes a practice of playing them whenever he has the opportunity, his game will suffer.

—HARRY VARDON, winner of a record six British Opens

The strengths of my game were developed in the States. As a student, I found the weather and the facilities were so good that I wanted to practice seven days a week. I put in a helluva lot of effort in college. I wasn't born with this ability. I had to work bloody hard to become the player I am today.

—COLIN MONTGOMERIE, one of Europe's best golfers

To score better, you must replicate on-course conditions as much as possible. For example, when practicing putter or bunker play, play one ball until you hole out. By moving around, changing clubs and lies, and playing from wherever the shot ends up, you are forced to make the shots necessary to get up-and-down on the course.

—PIA NILSSON, coach of the Swedish National Golf Team, *Golf Magazine* (1997)

I had to learn how to play out of bunkers because I used to be in so many of them.

—KEN VENTURI, winner of the 1964 U.S. Open

I chased pretty girls to a limited degree when I was serving my apprenticeship, but not excessively. When I was 17 and training for the Arkansas State Open, I wouldn't let myself date but once a week. I did gamble as a young man but I stopped when I got married. As a kid I just had to work too hard to fool around. My father had a dairy farm. I had to help with the milking in the mornings and evenings. And because I wanted to practice my golf, I needed my rest.

—PAUL RUNYON, winner of the 1938 PGA Championship and twenty-seven other PGA Tour events

I'd probably been up to 250, but I just happened to be at 215 at the time. I'd probably be the fat lady in a circus right now if it hadn't been for golf. It kept me on the course and out of the refrigerator.

—KATHY WHITWORTH, winner of a record 88 LPGA Tour events, on her portly youth

When practising, use the club that gives you the most trouble, and do not waste your time in knocking a ball about with the tool that gives you the most satisfaction and with which you rarely make a bad stroke.

—HARRY VARDON, from *The Complete Golfer*

It is strange how few bunkers one gets into during pretournament rounds, but in the competition proper they have a habit of almost springing up in the night. So bunker shot practice is very important to test the texture and depth of the sand.

—BILL COX, "Six Pointers to Better Golf," in *Secrets of the Golfing Greats*

Once you play in a tournament, you really get hooked on practice.

—BETSY RAWLS, four-time winner of the U.S. Women's Open

Most people want to spend all their time on the golf course, but if they want to be good players they're wasting their time. You've got to hit balls every day.

—Lee Trevino, winner of the U.S. Open in 1968 and 1971

———

I'm much better off by myself. When Jack Grout taught me to play, he taught me to correct myself. Frankly, I've probably had too many teachers. Lately, I'm better off by myself. I've got more gurus as far as my swing, health and fitness. I'd get home and have twelve phone calls to return.

—Jack Nicklaus in 1994

Don't swing the club, let the club swing you.

—LESLIE NIELSEN, from the video *Bad Golf My Way*

———

When you're down to four or five balls, put the driver away and try for two good shots with a wedge. Once you've hit your two, pick the other balls up and go home.

—TOM PAXSON, golf professional

They might be able to beat me, but they can't out-practice me.

—JERRY BARBER, journeyman PGA tour professional

———◆◆◆◆———

Practice is not to take the place of teaching, but to make teaching worthwhile.

—HARVEY PENICK, instructor to Tom Kite, Ben Crenshaw and other stars

I was all right teaching kids and beginners because they will listen. It's the 15-handicappers with bad grips who won't. Maybe if I charged them $500 an hour they would, but I couldn't so I told them to bugger off.

—SIMON HOBDAY, PGA Senior Tour Player, explaining why he stopped being a club professional in the 1980s.

First thing you have to do is get a room with black-out curtains. Start with full wedge shots. The window won't break. You can pretty much go through your short irons and not break the window.

—ANDREW MAGEE, PGA Tour player, on practicing in motel rooms

It is surely a curious fact that, though these three players dominated golf for so long, and the golfer is essentially an imitative animal, no one of them has been the founder of a school. They made people play better by having to live up to their standard, but they did not make people play like them.

—BERNARD DARWIN, British golf journalist, commenting on the Triumvirate: Braid, Taylor and Vardon, collectively winners of 16 British Opens

———◆•••◆———

Golf is a constant battle against par, and if you play it any other way, you are encouraging sloppy thinking and sloppy strokes. Ignore the social or business engagement on the golf course, therefore, and play medal whenever possible.

—GARY PLAYER, in *Secrets of the Golfing Greats*

I worked as hard to perfect my golf game as any other fellow would work in his brokerage office, in his job as a mechanic in a garage, as a lawyer or as a traveling salesman. My game was my business and as a business it demanded constant playing in the championship bracket, for a current title was my selling commodity.

—WALTER HAGEN, in his autobiography *The Walter Hagen Story*

I don't know why you're practicing so hard to finish second.

—BABE ZAHARIAS, to LPGA players practicing before a tournament

Dig it out of the ground like I did.

—BEN HOGAN, in response to a request for instruction

All golfers at some time or another get to the stage where they feel that they have reached the limit of their capabilities and that they cannot improve any further. . . . There is no way of telling yourself that this kind of streak will come to an end, it's just a matter of perseverance.

—GEORGE WILL, in *Good Advice for Men and Women Golfers*

Stick your butt out Mr. President.

—SAM SNEAD'S advice to President Eisenhower, when Ike asked why his swing was restricted

In addition to preparing the mind, you must prepare the muscles for a round of golf. The average golfer claims he hasn't the time to warm up, when the truth is he won't make or take the time. A four-hour round of golf can certainly be preceded by ten or fifteen minutes on the practice tee. By simply hitting a dozen balls you have eliminated three or four bad holes from your system. If you won't hit practice shots, at least swing something heavy before driving off.

—JACK BURKE, JR.

I have never been a heavy practicer from the stand-point of just beating balls. I thought hitting balls in preparation for playing and finding out how your swing was working, was practice. Sometimes that would take me 30 or 45 minutes. Sometimes it would take me six or seven hours. I never went out with a time schedule or with the idea to beat 500 balls.

—JACK NICKLAUS, winner of 18 major professional tournaments, *Golf Digest* (1991)

———

Thank God! Now, I'll never have to practice again.

—DOROTHY GERMAIN PORTER, in 1977 after winning the U.S. Senior Women's Amateur

5

Equipment

FAR AND SURE.

—Motto on Willie Park's coat, Musselburgh red with
blue collar

———•••••———

Some virtue went out of the game with the advent
of the rubber-core but . . . it made for a pleasanter
and easier game.

—Bernard Darwin, commenting on the advent of the
Haskell ball over the gutta-percha at the beginning of
the 20th century

Do not be tempted to invest in a sample of each new golfing invention as soon as it makes its appearance. If you do you will only complicate and spoil your game and encumber your locker with much useless rubbish. Of course some new inventions are good, but it is usually best to wait a little while to see whether any considerable section of the golfing public approves of them before rushing to order one.

—HARRY VARDON, one of the first golf professionals to endorse equipment

The finale in freak putters has apparently not yet come, for after nearly every shape of iron, wood and aluminum had been exhausted in an effort to give golfers an implement that would hole a ball regardless of the player's skill, a Chicago professional has come to the front with a putter made of gaspipe.

—*NEW YORK TIMES* article, July 27, 1922

I never played with the gutta-percha, or gutty, of course, and had never heard of it. The rubber-cored ball went on the market in 1902, the year I was born. The first ball I played with, after I began to notice that there were different kinds, was a Haskell Whiz, a fascinating ball marked with a little blue circle. I liked it a lot, and then, being fickle, I fancied the Dunlop Bramble and the Zome Zodiac, the latter name apparently hypnotized me. . . .

—BOBBY JONES, four-time winner of the U.S. Open

In order to preserve the balance between power and the length of holes and in order to retain the special features of the game, the power of the ball should be limited.

—THE ROYAL & ANCIENT RULES OF GOLF COMMITTEE RECOMMENDATION IN 1919

The most important item was the plus fours, a kind of knickers that had to hang exactly right if they were to make the wearer look like Gene Sarazen or Walter Hagen, not like a guy who put on his mother's bloomers by mistake.

—RICHARD ARMOUR, in his book *Golf is a Four-Letter Word* (1962)

It's shocking because you don't expect it to happen. It's a weird feeling. Going up the fairway, I had to get another club out to make sure my hands felt a club head again. It feels like your next shot, the head is going to fly off. I wanted to get that out of my system as fast as possible.

> —TIGER WOODS, after the club head on his driver flew off in the first round of the 2000 AT&T Pebble Beach National Pro-Am

---

I had a fifteenth club in my bag this week. It was Harvey Penick.

> —BEN CRENSHAW, who won the 1995 Masters after serving as pallbearer for his mentor, Harvey Penick

I had been a test pilot for Foot Joys forever. I test their sixty-five-dollar alligator models to see if standing in them for long periods of time in a bar brings any serious harm. What effect spilling beer has on them.

—GEORGE LOW, expert putter and golf hustler

Nice clods Stadler. Did you get those at a Buster Brown fire sale?

—FUZZY ZOELLER, kidding Craig Stadler about his shoes

Look at those spoiled bastards. They don't know the value of a dollar.

— GENE SARAZEN, commenting on touring pros who dropped new balls rather than search for shots hit in the rough

Why do I wear a red sport shirt on Sundays? Well, if I play bad on the last round of a tournament and cut my throat, it blends.

— LEE TREVINO, early in his professional career

It seems to me the more loft there is on a club, the harder it is to play. Why, I don't know.

—BOBBY JONES, three-time winner of the British Open

———

The lofted club is the answer. It is difficult to control a ball with a straight-faced club. Only a few players can do it. The straight-faced club gains distance but it loses accuracy. . . .

—CRAIG WOOD, on why he didn't use a driver off the tee

Always use the club that takes the least out of you. Play with a long iron instead of forcing your shot with a short iron. Never say, "Oh, I think I can reach it with such and such a club." There ought never to be any question of your reaching it, so use the next more powerful club in order that you will have a little in hand.

—HARRY VARDON, winner of the U.S. Open in 1900

Clubs meant nothing to Rolland. He had two or three of them tied round with a bit of string.

—RALPH SMITH, commenting on Douglas Rolland, big hitter among late 19th century British golf professionals

We had to wear long skirts, or course, and they were rather a nuisance. You took care they were not wider than they needed to be or they would swirl in the wind. And we didn't want them narrower than necessary because they would be constricting. The result was that our clothes looked alike, like uniforms. A continental woman once showed up in black trousers—they were not called slacks then. We were shocked. I guess we were surprised and more scandalized.

—JOYCE WETHERED, dominant player of the 1920s, commenting on women's attire in her era

How on earth any of us managed to hit a ball, in the outrageous garments which fashion decreed we should wear, is one of the great unsolved mysteries. I wore all grades of the stiff collar, first the plain stand up, then the double collar, highly glazed and as deep as possible. Often one got a raw sore neck all around the left side after playing in those monstrosities. Every self-respecting woman had to have a waist, and the more wasplike the more it was admired. This was a terrible drawback for golf . . .

—MABEL STRINGER, pioneer British lady golfer

No one would ever believe that any man ever played with that club in an international match.

—JOHN WARD, former major league baseball player and 1922 Walker Cup umpire, commenting on Bernard Darwin's spoon-like brassie at that first Walker Cup contest

You better use a putter cover, because you can put a dent in the face just by breathing on it.

> —BOBBY GRACE, golf club designer, discussing his "Fat Lady Swings" soft-faced putter

With wooden shafts you could stay on the ball longer. The club face stayed with the ball longer- that is, the ball did not leave it so quickly. You retained the feel longer. The ball didn't spring away from you.

> —JOYCE WETHERED, described by Bobby Jones as the best golfer he had ever seen, explaining the difference between steel-shafted and hickory shafted clubs

I'm sure this looks like I'm all over the charts, but it's what works out best for me. I test each club to find my personal preference, so there's a little bit of trial and error involved.

—LOREN ROBERTS, 1994 U.S. Open runner-up, on why he carries clubs from several manufacturers in his bag

———

The gutta-percha ball made all the difference to golf because the game would have dried out if a cheaper ball hadn't come in. The feather ball cost three to five shillings, which made it more expensive than the club. A man could only make three of them a day. . .

—BOBBY BURNET, club librarian of the Royal & Ancient on golf technology

You begin to get the idea that maybe golf manufacturers are out of control when you find out they are making clubs and balls out of components used in nuclear weapons and bulletproof vests.

—E. M. Swift, sports writer, on modern-day equipment

Always use a clean ball, and carry a sponge to keep it clean. It detracts from the pleasure of a game more than you may imagine if your ball is always dirty and cannot be seen from a distance. Besides, the eye is less strained when a clean white ball is played with, and there is less likelihood of foozled strokes. Moreover, your dirty ball is a constant irritation to your opponent.

—Harry Vardon, from his book *The Complete Golfer*

We're in America aren't we? If people want to buy a Chevy or Cadillac, they should be able to buy one. If you can build a better golf club, you should build it. When a lot of us are having trouble hitting the ball 220, or 120 yards, why should we be punished because Greg Norman can hit it 320 yards?

—KARSTEN SOLHEIM, founder of Ping and opponent of some USGA restrictions on equipment design

6

The Mental Game

I was young and righteous, but you cannot become a champion without the ability to cope with your emotions. That is the most important factor in becoming a winner. This is what it's all about—being able to control every emotion: elation, dejection, fear, greed, the whole lot.

—MICKEY WRIGHT, winner of the 1952 U.S. Girl's Junior

You seem to forget that luck is a part of the game and a good golfer must be good at all parts of the game.

—WALTER TRAVIS, three-time winner of the U.S. Amateur (1900–01, 1903), when it was suggested to him that he lost the U.S. Amateur because of an opponent's luck

Train yourself to accept the fact that as a human being you are prone to mistakes. Take pride in being emotionally resilient and mentally tough.

—DR. BOB ROTELLA, sports psychologist

I don't even know if there was a Mulligan. But he gave his name to a wonderful gesture—letting you play a bad first drive over, and no penalty.

—REX LARDNER, writer, in his book *Out of the Bunker and into the Trees*

———————

Set a thief to catch a thief. Set the mind to watch the mind it becomes in moments of excitement full of fancies, fears or useless wandering ideas and it may be no easy task to tie it down to the matter at hand . . . If the mind is full of fear or failure—a dread of the next approach, a persistent thought of three putts although the green is still far away— then, in my experience, there is but one thing that can at all help and that is to see the humor of the situation.

—JOYCE WETHERED, seven-time winner of the Worplesdon Foursomes (1922–23, 1927–28, 1931–33, 1936)

From a quiet house or a secluded part of a hotel, she would come to the first tee, smile charmingly at her opponent when they met at the commencement of their game, and then, almost as though in a trance, become a golfing machine . . . This cloak of inhumanity was not created to frighten the enemy; it served to conceal an intense concentration, and to conserve its owner's physical strength.

—ENID WILSON, golf journalist, on Joyce Wethered

To play well you must feel tranquil and at peace. I have never been troubled by nerves in golf because I felt I had nothing to lose and everything to gain.

—HARRY VARDON, member of the Golf Hall of Fame

Of all the hazards, fear is the worst.

—SAM SNEAD

———•••••———

The longer a club is the harder it is to get back to the ball after you've taken the clubhead away. And the more upright you are, the less chance there is of error. Carol Mann, JoAnne Carner, and Kathy Whitworth should beat me every time. They should be able to repeat the swing more consistently than I do but because I work harder, I am more consistent. There are people better coordinated than I am and with more ability, but if I had to choose, I'd take somebody with confidence over somebody with natural talent.

—SANDRA PALMER, LPGA pro, in "Sandra Palmer Can Handle the Pressure" by Sarah Ballard, *Sports Illustrated* (1975)

The only problem in major golf is, as ever "how to score," for nearly all the players setting out on the circuits can hit the ball. That is no problem. It is the scoring which counts. I think that to score in golf is a matter of confidence, if you think you cannot do it, then there is no chance that you will.

—HENRY COTTON

The point is that it doesn't matter if you look like a beast before or after the hit, as long as you look like a beauty at the moment of impact.

—SEVE BALLESTEROS, winner of two Masters (1980, 1983) and three British Opens (1979, 1984, 1988)

Concentration is not an element that should be applied all the way around a golf course. It is not the least bit important until you are ready to shoot. There's plenty of time to concentrate when you step up to the ball.

—JULIUS BOROS, in his book *How to Play Par Golf*

It [championships] is something like a cage. First you are expected to get into it and then you are expected to stay there. But of course, nobody can stay there. Out you go—and then you are trying your hardest to get back in again. Rather silly isn't it, when golf—just golf—is so much fun?

—BOBBY JONES, explaining why he retired from major competitive golf in 1930 at age 28

In his most youthful and tempestuous days he had never been angry and not often, I think, with Fate, but he had been furiously angry with himself. He set himself an almost impossibly high standard; he thought it an act of incredible folly if not a positive crime to make a stroke that was not exactly as it ought to be made. If he ever derogated from that standard he may even in his most mature days have been "mad" in the recesses of his heart, but he became outwardly a man of ice, with the very best of golfing manners.

—BERNARD DARWIN, on Bobby Jones in *The Darwin Sketch Book*

The bored haughty face that she turned to the world concealed something—most affectations concealed something eventually, even though they don't in the beginning—and one day I found out what it was. . . . At her first big golf tournament there was a row that nearly reached the newspapers—a suggestion that she had moved her ball from a bad lie in the semi-final round.

—F. SCOTT FITZGERALD, in *The Great Gatsby* (1925)

Every game of golf that has ever been played—whether the medal was 68 of 168—has taken place on a golf course that measured eight inches or less. I arrived at the dimensions of this golf course by taking a ruler and measuring my own head from back to front.

—EDDIE LOOS, American golf professional and teacher

It was kind of a process of self-isolation, of going into a shell, of putting away outside things. Crack American women golfers are adept at it. They brought it to the point of perfection. They never talk ... they seem to press a button and all at once, in their own minds, nobody else exists.

—PAM BARTON, British golfer, preparing for the 1936 U.S. Womens Amateur

The greedy golfer will go to near and be sucked into his own destruction.

—JOHN L. LOW, Scottish amateur golfer, golf writer and architect

Perhaps the best explanation is that Mac was harried in these events by some psychic injury sustained in his first mishaps that, fed by his subsequent failure to produce in the Opens, grew into a complex of such obstinate proportions that the harder he fought to defeat it, the more viciously it defeated him.

—HERBERT WARREN WIND, writer, on why Macdonald Smith couldn't win the big ones

If profanity had an influence on the flight of the ball, the game of golf would be played far better than it is.

—HORACE G. HUTCHINSON, British golfer and pioneer golf writer

It got worse and worse. It got to where I just hated to go out to the golf course because I knew I couldn't play anymore. There was panic and fear because I didn't know where the ball was going or whether I'd even hit it! To actually fear playing golf after having done so well is a terrible experience.

—KATHY WHITWORTH, winner of 88 LPGA events, describing what it was like to be in a slump

The average golfer, I can say flatly, lacks the ability to concentrate, which probably is the most important component of any good game. I believe the ability to concentrate is the difference in skill between the club player and the golf professional, even more than the shot-making process.

—DOW FINSTERWALD

Jack Nicklaus, when one of the brightest amateur stars, won a major championship without using anything longer than a six-iron for his second shots on par-four holes and was home in two on the majority of par fives with an iron. Nicklaus not only enjoys a tremendous advantage percentage-wise but also holds a substantial psychological edge over his opponents with his long ball.

—ARNOLD PALMER, in *Arnold Palmer's Golf Book*

I find a better way to let it go. I do something physical to feel better, like slam the club in the rough, slam my bag, or slap a tree.

—TOM LEHMAN, PGA professional

Golf is really three games. There's the long game, where women are at a disadvantage. There's the short game, where women are at no disadvantage at all; in fact, if they've worked on their coordination and perception, they are ahead of that game by a mile. And there is the game that is eighteen holes in one. Each hole is a miniature golf game, and individual challenge, an individual chance to "feel" the pitfalls of the course and attempt to beat the odds. Women are marvelous at this kind of thinking.

—LOUISE SUGGS

When I left the course after a round this year, a lady told me my biorythms were off. I told her my golf game was off.

—JACK NICKLAUS, winner of at least one PGA tournament for seventeen consecutive years (1962–78), in 1978

When we first arrived, some of the players were talking about how nervous they were. I squelched that right away. I want no negativity. I wanted everything and everybody up. I told them if they were nervous I would get them some vaseline for their teeth to quiet the chattering noise.

—JoANNE CARNER, captain of the victorious 1994 U.S. Solheim Cup team

Instead of putting pressure on myself and thinking, "I've got to make this shot," I just thought, "Go ahead and make it." It's a subtle difference but a big one.

—COREY PAVIN, after sinking a 141-yard 9-iron shot at a critical point in the 1993 Ryder Cup

The loss of enthusiasm—I think that happens to everybody when they don't play well. I'm not one of those guys who can be confident and happy when they're not playing well. It got to be a vicious circle. I wasn't playing well, so I wasn't confident.

> —CURTIS STRANGE, explaining his slump after winning back-to-back U.S. Opens in 1988 and 1989

You go out and play your game. Sometimes it comes out as 68 and sometimes at 74. That's not fatalism, that's golf.

> —PETER OOSTERHUIS, after being criticized as "fatalistic" rather than assertive on the professional tour

Imagine what it was like for me. One day it's John Philip Sousa marches and razor sharp creases in my whites. I'm the All-American boy, blond and bright. The next day I'm in a padded cell in a straight jacket. They gave me a series of six shock treatments in three months.

> —BERT YANCEY, former PGA Tour player, describing the start of his manic depression while a West Point cadet in 1960

I love to watch "Oprah," "Geraldo," all the shows about dysfunctionals. That's my psychoanalysis. I realized I wasn't as bad as I thought.

> —MAC O'GRADY, PGA Tour professional

I feel my composure is a hundred percent better now than, say, a year ago. I think our galleries enjoy seeing some emotion from the players. I don't think there's anything wrong with showing your temper as long as you don't damage the course or do something to disturb another player. Too many of our players are like robots.

—BETH DANIEL, in 1980, her second year on the LPGA Tour, commenting after being fined for club-throwing

I get pissed off. I simply do not understand someone who hits a ball that lands behind a tree and can look at and say, "Well, that's golf."

—SIMON HOBDAY, Senior Tour pro, on how he reacts to a bad shot

I motivate myself by thinking of my family. If I can't be with them at home, I'd rather make my time out here worthwhile. If I play well, I feel like I can justify being away from them—it's okay to leave them that week. If I don't play well, then I feel like I've wasted time I could have spent with them.

—NANCY LOPEZ, LPGA Hall of Famer and mother of three

I was so nervous today I was almost jumping out of my skin all day. Usually when I'm playing decent, I'm nervous.

—TOM WATSON on winning the 1981 Masters

Anyone who rode to the Wentworth Club with the American team on their way to play the International Team Match against Great Britain would never state that a top-class golfer has no nerves. Nervousness is shown in various ways, depending upon the temperament of a person. I do not know how many of the girls noticed this during that short ride, but it was apparent to me. Some were talking incessantly, others not saying a word. The majority of us were yawning, a true sign of nervousness. I dare say none of us were quite sure what we had eaten for breakfast.

—VIRGINIA VAN WIE, American golf champion, in 1934

We have to be pretty self-centered and confident in ourselves to be successful on the Tour. We have strong personalities—maybe even more so than other professions—because we have to depend solely on our own abilities. My faith has tempered that self-centered streak and helped me to look beyond my own needs to the needs of others.

> —BETSY KING, in 1994, after becoming a Christian golfer

That way you can understand why you're driving yourself crazy.

> —ALLISON FINNEY, LPGA professional, explaining why she majored in psychology

We've lost our national way. We are a society of Chip Becks laying up intelligently.

—TOM CALLAHAN, writer, commenting on modern American golf in 1995

———•◦•———

Yeah. I think when I play golf, yes, I think I have to make the world revolve around me. If you want to be the best at something, you have to make it revolve around what you are doing. Is that clear?

—JACK NICKLAUS, in a *Golf Digest* interview in 1991

Golf is in the interest of good health and good manners. It promotes self-interest and affords a chance to play the man and act the gentleman.

—WILLIAM HOWARD TAFT, the first U.S. President to play serious golf

7

Swings

A golf swing is a collection of corrected mistakes.

—CAROL MANN, winner of 38 LPGA events

———◆•❖•◆———

Long swing, long career.
Short swing, short career.

—JACK BURKE, JR., member of the PGA Hall of Fame

His wriggling at the address has been likened to a man squirming his way into a telephone box with a load of parcels in his arms.

—RALPH GULDAHL'S swing described in *The Encyclopedia of Golf* (1975)

It comes and it goes. It's the kind of thing you can't turn loose once you've got it going or it might never come back.

—CRAIG WOOD, commenting on the elusiveness of a grooved golf swing prior to the 1941 U.S. Open

The golfing public has, in the last few decades, been steered away from golf as a game of feel. The emphasis today is on the mechanics of the swing. As you may have already noticed, I think this is the wrong path.

—JIM FLICK, noted golf instructor, in a 1997 *Golf Magazine* article

He didn't know enough about the swing to come back.

—GEORGE FAZIO, on Ralph Guldhal's inability to change from being an instinctual golfer who couldn't correct his mistakes

If ah didn't have these ah'd hit it twenty yards farther.

> —BABE ZAHARIAS, describing how her breasts impeded her golf swing

———

JoAnne has a swing like Babe (Zaharias) did. JoAnne has the power that Babe had and the same sort of three-quarter swing. She also had the Babe's communication with her galleries.

> —MARILYN SMITH, on JoAnne Gunderson Carner's swing

. . . a fidgety player who addressed the ball as if he could reason with it.

> —A characterization of President Woodrow Wilson's golf game

---

. . . even God can't hit a 1-iron.

> —LEE TREVINO, suggesting that holding a 1-iron aloft might protect a golfer from lightning in a thunderstorm

At this meeting, it was possible for the serious-minded to make a comparison between the English and Scottish swings, and the opinion was the Scottish swings were quicker and shorter.

—From the minutes of a meeting of The First Ladies' Golf Union in 1895

The golfer's left side must be the dominant part of the swing. This is the only way to get maximum power and accuracy. If the right side takes over, there is no golf swing.

—KATHY WHITWORTH, LPGA Hall of Famer

I didn't put myself in the thought process to realize that the lie would automatically come off there a little bit left. Well, when you cut across from that kind of lie (downhill, sidehill), it starts it to the left. That's exactly what I did. It started about a yard and a half in the water and it just went dead straight. It was a good shot, but it was a bad mental mistake.

—RAYMOND FLOYD, describing how an errant 7-iron on the 11th at Augusta, cost him a chance at victory in a playoff against Nick Faldo in the 1990 Masters

. . . a physicist can describe the perfect golf swing and write it down in scientific language, but the smart golfer doesn't read it. The smart golfer gives it his opponent to contemplate.

—DR. FRAN PIROZOLLO, sports psychologist

I sometimes lose control of my emotions so completely, that I don't know where I am or that it's me hitting the ball.

—MICKEY WRIGHT, winner of 82 tournaments on the LPGA Tour, during her early years

The shank—of all the golfing diseases, shanking is by far the most outrageous in its devastating results.

—ROGER WETHERED, from *The Game of Golf* (1931)

I found that seeing the swinge of your body by turning it upon your legge is the largest and strongest motion. Therefor it must begin first and the turning at the small of the back must only second it, and then must follow the motion at the shoulders.

—THOMAS KINCAID, from his diary in *The Book of the Old Edinburgh Club* (1687)

What I mean is, that you must not begin the downward swing as if you were anxious to get it over. Haste spells disaster and disaster is disheartening. I am always on the look-out against a pupil becoming downhearted.

—ALEXANDER "SANDY" HERD, British golfer and instructor

The real road to improvement lies in gaining a working understanding of the correct swing in general, and of his own swing in particular. When he has done this, there will be something on which to hang his concentration. Then he will have some chance of learning what to think about instead of finding himself in utter confusion over half a hundred details as he stands up to start his stroke.

—BOBBY JONES, winner of four U.S. Opens, five U.S. Amateurs, three British Opens, and one British Amateur

I don't like mechanics. The best swing is the one with the least mechanics. When you see George Duncan or Harry Vardon or Bobby Jones swing, do you notice any mechanics? I don't want my pupils to bother their heads about mechanics, or which hand takes the club up, and which sends it down.

—STEWART MAIDEN, golf professional and instructor of Bobby Jones, Alexa Stirling and others

Readers are reminded that the word "yip" was invented by T. D. Armour the great teacher of golf . . . Armour defines "yips" as a "brain spasm which impairs the short game." "Impairs" is a euphemism.

—STEPHEN POTTER, in his book *Golfsmanship* (1968)

I simply swing at the ball with the one idea of hitting it. I knew nothing of the golf theory mind you, I already had won ten national championships. Why, I was nineteen years old before I first heard the golfing terms "pull" and "slice." The old idea was to hit the ball—few attempts were made at theorizing—and I'm not too sure it wasn't a blessed good idea.

—DOROTHY CAMPBELL HURD, winner of 11 major championships and the first British-born player to win the U.S. Women's Amateur

Don't you wish you could hit the ball like that?

—BABE ZAHARIAS, winner of 31 LPGA events, demonstrating how to drive at a golf clinic

Long driving is of prime importance in golf. It need not be long enough to give the golfer some chance against par, and to put him on good terms with himself.

—TED RAY, winner of the British Open (1912) and the U.S. Open (1920)

Bob Hope's swing? I've seen better swings on a condemned playground.

—BING CROSBY, singer and founder of the PGA Bing Crosby Pro-Am

I may go for it, and I may not. It all depends what I elect to do on my backswing.

—BILLY JOE PATTON, in the 1954 Masters

Jones: Mr. Vardon, did you ever see a worse shot than that?

Vardon: No.

—HARRY VARDON's reply to Bobby Jones when he skulled a niblick in the 1920 U.S. Open

Never saw one who was worth a damn.

—HARRY VARDON, 1900, commenting on left-handed golfers

Harry Vardon was a big man with huge hands. My own was practically lost in his hand shake. He was reserved, quiet, with almost nothing to say. But I learned plenty from watching him swing a golf club. He had a much more compact and precise swing than I had ever seen. He had it in a groove and I tried it out in practice and it worked for me too.

—WALTER HAGEN, observing Harry Vardon at the 1913 U.S. Open at The Country Club

If your swing was good enough to win one out there, it's good enough to win again. Your problem isn't usually your swing. It's your heart.

—MARK McCUMBER, winner of over $4 million on the PGA tour

I didn't want to (shoot for the pin) but there's this thing in my brain that just shoved the ball over there.

> —FRED COUPLES, explaining how he almost hit a tee shot into Rae's Creek on the 12th hole in the final round of his 1992 Masters win

Flat-footed golf, sir, flat-footed golf.

> —J. H. TAYLOR, winner of five British Opens, describing his golf technique

A mis-hit. She caught it and it just rolled and rolled.

—Mic Potter, Furman University Coach, commenting
on All-American Caroline Peek's winning 278-yard
smash in the 1992 NCAA Championship long drive
contest

———

Mine was, and remains, almost the antitheses of a
"mechanical" golf swing. . . . Pap's basic premise was
that once you learned the proper grip and under-
stood the fundamental motion behind the swing,
the trick was to find the swing that worked best for
you and your body type, maximized your power.
The rest of it was a lifelong learning process of refinement by trial and error.

—Arnold Palmer, in his autobiography *A Golfer's Life*
(1999) with James Dodson

If you must, let your practice swing be the one where you think of mechanics. Once your mechanics feel right, take a trial swing to concentrate on the target and the feel.

—DR. BOB ROTELLA, sports psychologist

In using the word rhythm I am not speaking of the swing. The rhythm I have reference to here could also be described as the order of procedure. Walter Hagen was probably the greatest exponent of the kind of rhythm I have in mind to play golf.

—BEN HOGAN, in his book *Power Golf* (1948)

. . . Her swing was not pretty to watch; it was incredibly flat compared with modern teaching. She used the palm grip with her right hand very much under the shaft. This and her straight left arm, always stiff like a ramrod, gave her exceptional control and power over her iron shots. This style was her own distinctive method of attacking a golf ball from early childhood on.

—A GOLF JOURNALIST, describing Cecil Leitch, British Ladies' Champion and the first "power player" among women golfers

To reach the correct position at the top of the swing it is vital that the first movement should be correct. I can't stress that too strongly. Take the clubhead back all in one piece with the shoulders, arms, hands, and club moving together. This movement insures that you go back on the inside groove after the first few inches of the swing. If the club starts back on the outside it will be impossible to reach the right position at the top of the swing, so you can see how important this first take-away movement is to good golf.

—DAI REES, British professional golfer in *Secrets of the Golfing Greats*

The golf swing is a knack requiring the unselfconsciousness and the confidence with which people bicycle or swim. Such skills are only acquired by associating certain movements with particular effects, and only after innumerable falls and swallowing a considerable amount of water.

—ENID WILSON, British golfer and journalist

I think my swing has been on the upright side probably through the years. But these guys who play by mechanical means with positions, I don't see how they can even play golf doing that. I have always felt you have to play golf by feel. All athletes, when they get in pressure situations, revert to what they know. I don't think you are going to revert to mechanics. I think you revert to feel.

—JACK NICKLAUS, in *Golf Digest* (1991)

It was a very lonely life. But making a change in a golf swing takes a long time, and winter is time for making changes. You do it over and over again, and it is so long before you can see the change that you sometimes wonder why you are doing it at all.

—SANDRA PALMER, in "Sandra Palmer: She Can Handle The Pressure" by Sarah Ballard in *Sports Illustrated* (1975)

I accept the fact that I'm going to miss it sometimes. I just hope I miss it where I can find it.

—FUZZY ZOELLER, winner of the 1979 Masters and the 1984 U.S. Open

What helped me more than anything at this point in my career was a remark Alexa Sterling made to me one day on the first tee. She said that at the top of my swing with the driver—and, I presume, with all clubs—the face of the club was pointing upward. This had not caused most of the unsteadiness in my driving. I immediately corrected this fault by keeping my left wrist under the shaft at the top of the swing. Another thing: I found that my backswing was almost as fast as my downswing. By slowing it down, I gained a great deal more control.

—GLENNA COLLETTE, from her book *Ladies in the Rough* (1928)

On the fairway many golfers have a tendency to try and lift the ball into the air, and in doing so, they lift their body on the downswing as though their arms were going to pick the ball up and send it away. But the only way to get a ball in the air is to hit down into it. The loft of the club, plus the down-and-through motion of the downswing gets the ball in the air and makes it impossible to top it.

—JOHNNY FARRELL, from *Secrets of the Golfing Greats*

I just vomit when I hear 'em talk about the bump-and-run because you just can't do it here.

—PETE DYE, golf course designer, commenting on how the bump-and-run shot has been eliminated by heavily watered fairways on U.S. golf courses

. . . he [I] just happened to be hitting just the right sort of ball for the day.

> —JOHN BALL, eight-time winner of the British Amateur, explaining how he won a medal competition in the wind at Hoylake

Imagine a short man (he is five feet six inches in height) with a long club placing his feet with meticulous care in regard to line and then rather sitting down on the ball. The waggle is careful and restrained; then suddenly all is changed; he seems almost to jump on his toes in the upswing and fairly flings himself into the ball.

> —BERNARD DARWIN, describing Harold Hilton, winner of two British Opens, three Irish Opens, three British Amateurs and one U.S. Amateur

Some years ago, quite a little publicity was given to the fact that Miss Helen Hicks used wood clubs with the word "oompah" stamped on the head. She explained that she allowed this word, with the first syllable dwelt upon, to run through her mind as she was getting ready to play a stroke to improve her sense of timing.

—BOBBY JONES, commenting on the technique of Helen Hicks

I have a hook. It nauseated me. I could vomit when I see one. It's like a rattlesnake in your pocket.

—BEN HOGAN, winner of 9 major golf tournaments

8

Putting

Hitting a golf ball and putting have nothing in common. They are two different games. You work all of your life to perfect a repeating swing that will get you to the greens, and then you have to try to do something that is totally unrelated. There shouldn't be any cups, just flagsticks. And then the man who hit the most fairways and greens and got closest to the pins would be the tournament winner.

> —BEN HOGAN, in his later years, when he couldn't make a putt

I swear that ball saw more lip than Bianca Jagger on her wedding night. But the kiss never came.

> —PETER JACOBSEN, PGA Tour journeyman, lamenting a missed putt

Hell, I'd putt sitting up in a coffin if I thought I could hole something.

> —GARDNER DICKINSON, justifying his strange putting stance

Schenectady: A center-shafted putter with an aluminum head, patented by Arthur F. Knight of Schenectady, New York in 1903, used by Walter J. Travis in winning the British Amateur Championship in 1904, and shortly thereafter banned by the Royal & Ancient.

—PETER DAVIES, from *The Historical Dictionary of Golf* (1992)

———

To such a perfect putter as Mr. Travis, who would putt if need were with an umbrella or walking-stick, doubtless there are no difficulties.

—ARTHUR POLTOW, in the *Illustrated Outdoor News* (1906)

Putting is always the great equaliser, because if you are putting well then it takes a lot of pressure off the rest of your game. You can afford to make a few mistakes if you're holing ten- and fifteen-footers for par.

—Tom Watson, in 1999, remembering when he won the 1975 British Open at Carnoustie

The devoted golfer is an anguished soul who has learned a lot about putting just as an avalanche victim has learned a lot about snow.

—Dan Jenkins, noted American golf writer

To many, Bolt's putter has spent more time in the air than Lindbergh.

> —JIMMY DEMARET, commenting on the club-throwing habits of Tommy Bolt

On the putting green the mind can be a grave source of trouble. Begin to dislike the look of a putt, and the chances of holing it at once become less.

> —JOYCE WETHERED, four time winner of the British Ladies' Championship (1922, 1924–25, 1929)

When hitting an approach putt, try to lay the ball into an imaginary three-foot circle around the hole. I feel a definite hit with my right hand on both long and short putts. I recommend a rather long and un-hurried backswing in putting because it makes the stroke smoother and eliminates the putting yips which sometimes besets golfers who have short, compact backswings.

—BILLY CASPER, member of the PGA Hall of Fame

Forget the idea of a three-foot target area around the hole on long putts. Archers and pistol shooters aim for bulls-eyes, not the outer circles. Aim to make the putt.

—DR. BOB ROTELLA, sports psychologist

Fact one: anyone with normal coordination can become the best putter in the world. Fact two: great putting can make up for many other faults during a round. But no one putts well day-in and day-out if they don't first believe they are a great putter.

—Pia Nilsson, coach of the Swedish National Golf Team

The more you miss, the worse it gets. The worse it gets, the more likely you are to miss again.

—Dave Pelz with James A. Frank, from the article "You Need a Ritual," *Golf Magazine* (1997)

Best player I ever saw in any capacity for a period of about five or six years was Tom Watson. By that I mean Thursday, Friday, Saturday and Sunday under the gun. He was phenomenal. Over a career I think Jack Nicklaus has been by far, the best at making the crucial putt. Then you've got George Archer and Bob Charles, guys who wherever they were, you expected them to make it . . . Dave Stockton has always been a fabulous putter under the gun.

—RAYMOND FLOYD, assessing the game's best putters in 1994

I might practice a half-hour sometimes. But I never practiced when I was younger because it hurt my back. It doesn't take me very long to feel like I am putting the ball pretty well. Frankly, I find that when I lay off, the first thing that comes back is my putter. Not necessarily the attitude of good putting, but certainly my stroke. I think it takes a few tournaments before you can get back the attitude of making putts.

—JACK NICKLAUS in 1991

Ted's trouble was this. In Britain when the greens are terribly keen, they are brown. We don't water them there. Here, they were keen and slipping as ever they get in Britain; but they were green and the texture is apparently substantial. I never saw more lovely greens. But fast as lightning. And Ted, for all his superb touch, could never get himself in the mood to realize he was putting over racing greens. That's the reply.

—GEORGE DUNCAN, 1920 British Open winner, commenting on Ted Ray and Oakmont's greens in the 1927 U.S. Open

I think I have a real good stroke, I really do, but I swear, I'm the queen of the lip-out and the rim-out. The ball comes out and looks up at me and grins, as if to say "too bad, you missed again." I just don't know how to die the ball into the cup.

—PAT BRADLEY, winner of 31 LPGA, in 1979, at the age of 28

That shot cost me the championship.

—JOCK HUTCHINSON'S comment on his missed three-foot putt for birdie on the 69th hole at Inverness in the 1920 U.S. Open

If I could just putt. I might just scare somebody, maybe me.

> —JACK NICKLAUS, after two rounds of the 1986 Masters, which he won a record sixth time

I made that putt. It just didn't go in.

> —TOM KITE, explaining his missed 12-footer on the 72nd hole to lose by one stroke in the 1986 Masters

I had never seen or heard of a bent grass green before. I had played on sand greens and Bermuda, but these were frightening, slick and fast. I three-putted everything.

—BYRON NELSON, remembering his first experience with bent grass greens in the 1934 U.S. Amateur

Q: Thirteen? How the hell did you make 13 on a par-s?

Arnold Palmer: Missed a 12-footer for 12.

—ARNOLD PALMER, explaining how he made a 12 in the 1961 Los Angeles Open

I putt so bad I'm gonna eat a can of Alpo.

—LEE TREVINO during a tournament in 1975

———•••••———

Put me on a putting green in Miami for a week and I'll kill more tourists than the Fountainbleau.

—GEORGE LOW, putting hustler

———•••••———

There are many ways to punish a putter, such as burning, rusting and drowning, but the most tortuous is to drag it along pavement out of the door of a fast-moving vehicle.

—DAN JENKINS, presenting one of his *Ten Basic Rules for Happy Putting*

9

Men Touring

When they made their appearance, the professional golfer here was apt to be a rather shiftless, feckless person—a pleasant enough fellow, but living from hand to mouth and not always to be relied upon. That he is today a respected and self-respecting, prosperous member of society is largely due to the generations of professionals which arose in the early nineties with J. H. as their natural born leader.

—BERNARD DARWIN, commenting on British golfer J. H. Taylor's impact on professional golf at the turn of the century.

The honorable Commisary and Magistrates of Fort Orange and the village of Beverwyck, having heard diverse complaints from the burghers of this place against the practice of playing golf along the streets, which causes great damage to the windows of the houses and also exposes people to the danger of being injured and is contrary to freedom of the public streets. Therefore their honors, wishing to prevent the same, hereby forbid all persons to play golf in the streets, under forfeiture of 25 florins for each person who shall be found doing so.

—An early ordinance against golf in 17th century colonial America

The feeling toward the golf professionals in this country was such that the winner of the 1898 U. S. Open, Fred Herd, was required to put up security for the safe keeping of the trophy. It was feared he would pawn the trophy for drinking money.

—AL BARKOW, American golf writer, on the early lack of respect for golf professionals

Pro golf is a parasitical business and they can do without us.

—WALTER HAGEN, winner of two U.S. Opens, five PGA Championships, and four British Opens

The fastest driver was Craig Wood. He had a 12-cylinder Packard, a big, long car with two seats. He was driving fast at night in Texas with Vic Ghezzi once and drove right under a horse. He was going so fast that it pitched the horse over the car, and it didn't hurt them. It killed the horse, but only damaged the front of the car.

—PAUL RUNYAN, describing travel on the pro circuit in the 1930s

If it were not for you Walter, this dinner would be downstairs in the pro shop and not in the ballroom.

—ARNOLD PALMER, to Walter Hagen, at a dinner in Hagen's honor in the 1960s

In those days, the money was the main thing, the only thing I played for. Titles were something to grow old with.

—BYRON NELSON, on playing to win in the 1937 Masters

I got my golfing education from the drubbings. And very lately I have come to a sort of Presbyterian attitude toward tournament golf; I can't get away from the idea of predestination.

—BOBBY JONES, in his autobiography *Down the Fairway*, published in 1927 when he was 25 years old

Expert golf is an art, not a trade, and unionization of players doesn't work.

> —BOB HARLOW, early PGA Tour Director, reacting to the organization of professionals in 1936

When a man stands alone on the tee, surrounded by galleries he knows hold him in awe because of his talent at the bewildering game of golf and also because of his willingness to risk abject failure right out in the open, he very easily, very naturally sees himself as a hero figure.

> —AL BARKOW, in his book *Golf's Golden Grind*

I decided to play some records on the phonograph to kill some time, things like Glenn Miller. I thought I played those records for hours. I was ready to throw the machine out the window. I checked the time and it was only 10 o'clock. Then I get out some magazines and read them for what seems like hours. At 11 o'clock I bathed and shaved and ate a big breakfast here at the club and killed time in the locker room and hit a few shots down the practice fairway, and then it was nearly 1:42. I thought it would never come.

—CARY MIDDLECOFF, describing his wait before the final round of the 1955 Masters, which he won

The only emotion Ben shows in defeat is surprise.
You see, he expects to win.

—JIMMY DEMARET, commenting on his friend Ben Hogan

If I can't play this last nine in thirty-seven strokes,
I'm just a bum and don't deserve to win the Open.

—RALPH GULDAHL'S thoughts at the turn before winning
the 1937 U.S. Open

My God. I've won the Open.

—KEN VENTURI, after winning the 1964 U.S. Open

Okay. But you better win this tournament . . . or else.

—LLOYD MANGRUM'S WIFE to her hubby before the 1946
U.S. Open, after catching Mangrum in bed with another
woman. Lloyd won the tournament

. . . Well, he wasn't married when he was on the Tour.

—BARBARA NICKLAUS, explaining a Tour player's demise

What a stupid I am.

—ROBERTO DE VICENZO after handing in an incorrect
scorecard which cost him a 1968 Master's win by one
stroke

I was tryin's to get so far ahead I could choke and still win, but I had to keep on playin'.

> —LEE TREVINO, on being chased by Jack Nicklaus in the 1968 U.S. Open. Trevino won with four subpar rounds.

If you don't shut up, I'm going to tell where you swam across the border.

> —DOUG SANDERS, to a talkative Lee Trevino at the Masters

Do you know how many times I've had some guy on a Toro lawnmower on my butt as the sun is going down and I'm trying to make a six-footer to make the cut?

—DENNIS TRIXLER, journeyman golfer

Whenever there are winners, there must be losers. In golf the winner is the man who brings in the lowest score, in stroke play, or who scores lower on more holes than his opponent, in match play. Nine times out of ten, scores are very just bases on which to judge the respective merits of golfers.

—HERBERT WARREN WIND, in his book *The Story of American Golf*

You're embarrassed. You're in a fog. You're standing in front of the world and it's like you're playing the hole naked.

> —TOM WIESKOPF, describing his thought processes on the way to a 13 on the 155-yard par-s twelfth at Augusta National in the 1980 Masters

When Christ arose God placed the Masters jacket on him.

> —SIGN AT THE WOODLAWN BAPTIST CHURCH IN AUGUSTA GEORGIA, 1972

I played 36 holes today with a kid who should have won this Open by ten shots.

> —BEN HOGAN, assessing Jack Nicklaus, a 20-year-old amateur who almost won the 1960 U.S. Open

———•••••———

I kept getting tears in my eyes. It happened to me once at Baltusrol. But here, it happened to me four or five times. I had to say to myself, Hey, you've got some golf to play.

> —JACK NICKLAUS, in the 1986 Masters

I finally found that guy I used to know on the golf course. It was me.

> —JACK NICKLAUS, after winning his sixth Masters in 1986, at the age of 46

But there is a constant truth about tournament golf. Other men have to lose a championship before one man can win it.

> —DAN JENKINS, golf writer

Golf pros, almost to a man are conservative. Perhaps this is forced on them by the game they play. Golf is a game of considered judgment, careful ball placement and strategy, the avoidance of hazards. Most who play are not prone to take chances.

—AL BARKOW, golf writer, commenting on the nature of the Tour

Tour professionals make their living shooting low scores and cannot afford risky shots ardent golfers love to try.

—PETE DYE, explaining why Tour players rebel against some of his courses such as PGA West and TPC Stadium at Sawgrass

I'm gonna be a Spaniard instead of a Mexkin as soon as I get some more money.

—LEE TREVINO, just before winning his first U.S. Open in 1968

I probably wouldn't have gone if not for the golf scholarship. Got to admit. I just walked through school as a conduit to the Tour.

—CHARLES COODY, regarding the merits of attending TCU

10

Women Touring

Indoor golf is to be one of the features of the athletic work of many young society girls this winter. They are the younger girls, hardly risen to the dignity of society "buds," but they have already been exposed to the contagion of golf, and they will prepare this winter to be genuine fanatics by the time their school duties are over.

—*THE NEW YORK TIMES*, November 14, 1897

My father had the Arabic attitude that, to enter heaven, he had got to have a son to close his eyes. When I arrived, he was displeased. And it was made known to me from word naught that, as a woman, I was inferior in every way. Fair enough. You know right where you are, right from the word go.

—ENID WILSON, three-time winner of the British Ladies'
(1931–33) and two time winner of the English Ladies'
(1928, 1930)

Nancy, I don't want the money if I have to make it this way. I want to live my life outdoors. I want to play golf.

—BABE ZAHARIAS, to her sister Esther Nancy, on deciding
to give up a $2,500-per-week Depression-era vaudeville
contract to play competitive golf

Then in 1940 I turned pro. I went with the Wilson sporting goods company. They offered me a job, and it was a very good arrangement. My father went to Chicago and discussed it with Mr. I. B. Icely, the president of Wilson. You know at that time you didn't have any managers, so your father was your manager, or at least helped you. My dad was the greatest.

—Patty Berg, pioneer on the LPGA Tour, from *Getting to the Dance Floor* by Al Barkow (1986)

Babe Zaharias was a remarkable person. She was no pantywaist, I'll tell you. She definitely was stronger than most men. When she walked, her muscles just rippled under her skin. She could hit it longer than I could; so could Mickey Wright.

—Paul Runyon, winner of 28 PGA tournaments

I worked for my money, why shouldn't they? Why should I support them now—if I get sick, are they going to feel an obligation to support me?

> —LOUISE SUGGS, LPGA professional, in 1961, expressing her opposition to sharing purses (5 percent) with golfers out of the money in a tournament

Those were great times. Our purses were meager by today's standards, but you could make a living of necessity, because we were always on the road and there were only a few dozen players. We were closer, too. After a tournament, we'd always sit around together and have a party. Usually the winner would buy the drinks because she was the only one who had any money.

> —KATHY WHITWORTH, LPGA Hall of Famer, recalling her early tour years in the late 1950s and early 1960s

I've seen it happen that one girl will help another who's having trouble with her swing, knowing that next week she may go out and beat her because of it. They'll come in after a round of a tournament and go back to watch somebody else play. They play against each other and they're playing to eat, and they come in and are good friends. I defy the men to do it, at least without a couple of shots of whiskey.

—BOB HAGGE, husband of LPGA player Marlene Bauer Hagge, comparing the PGA and LPGA tours in 1961

I found two sharks. They were washed up on the beach, and I tried to cut them open with my pocket knife, but they were too tough, so I took the car and ran over them, but that didn't work either. I mean I never saw the inside of a shark.

—CAROL MANN, LPGA golfer, recalling tour adventures along the Gulf of Mexico in the 1960s

I love golf, but I'm not going to sacrifice everything for the game. If some people want to, I think it's wonderful. But if I want to date, to stay out till three in the morning, I'm going to, and if I want to have a drink, I'm going to. I'm not going to stop talking to people because of golf. Some people get themselves in a trance on the course, but I may be thinking about my wash . . . It's a lot harder than some people think, waking up in the morning and you can't remember what town you're in.

—GLORIA ARMSTRONG, LPGA Professional, remembering life on the early LPGA Tour

I wonder what they think about women and children. They seem so lonely. Nothing to look forward to, to come home to.

—MURLE MACKENZIE, LPGA professional, commenting on the early LPGA Tour

Mickey had no touch at all on the chip shots, and she was absolutely the worst putter I have ever seen in competitive golf. Her mental attitude was all wrong. She was preoccupied with playing flawlessly from tee to green. If she didn't hit fifteen of the eighteen greens in regulation stroke, she was disgusted. She had complete contempt for scrambling. It took her at least two years to learn to respect the short game and realize that even the top players have to be able to get down in two from off the green. Then her chipping and putting started to improve, and, of course, her scoring did.

—BETSY RAWLS, LPGA contemporary of Mickey Wright, winner of 82 tournaments on the LPGA Tour

It is my belief that this attitude of aggressiveness is far more prevalent in competitive golf today than it used to be. It creates poor sportsmanship and spoils the joy of the game for the players and the pleasures of watching a shot-making game for the gallery.

—VIRGINIA VAN WIE, three-time U.S. Amateur champion (1932–34), commenting on women's competitive golf in *The American Golfer Magazine* (1934)

I remember making rulings on other players in a tournament I was competing in. In this day and age, you'd probably get sued for something like that.

—BETSY RAWLS, winner of 55 LPGA events and a member of the LPGA Hall of Fame, recalling the formative years of the Tour when she was an LPGA executive

Winning the Open is the greatest thing in golf. I have come close before. This time I'd thought I'd won. But I didn't. Golf is played by the rules, and I broke a rule. I've learned a lesson. And I have two broad shoulders.

> —JACKIE PUNG, after being disqualified in the 1957 U.S. Women's Open at Winged Foot where she reported a correct total score but recorded an incorrect score on one hole

I thought you had to be dead to win that.

> —JOANNE CARNER, LPGA Hall of Famer, in 1982, on winning the Bob Jones award for sportsmanship

Golf is my job and that motivates me. I have a talent.
I want to develop it. Every year I learn a different
shot. That's what great about golf. It's a very complex
game, very challenging. You never stop learning.

—BETSY KING, winner of over $5 million on the
LPGA Tour

———◆◆◆———

Well it just goes to show what we've been saying all
along. That all the good-looking golfers are on the
ladies' tour.

—JAN STEPHENSON, responding to a *Golf Magazine*
centerfold on male PGA Tour golfers

I felt something heavy. It was not that I was not feeling well. Maybe you could call it pressure.

> —AYAKO OKOMOTO, in 1988, after failing to win the Mazda-PGA Championship

Today was the best I've played in weeks. I didn't lose with bogeys. I lost to birdies, and that's the way you should lose.

> —BRANDIE BURTON, in 1989, after losing the U.S. Women's Amateur, 4 and 3, to Vicki Goetze at Pinehurst No. 2

I started in engineering and switched to business for my major. If I had stayed for my junior year, I'd have had to switch to basket weaving. It was getting tough.

> —NANCY LOPEZ, recalling how she left Tulsa University to join the LPGA Tour

Having a good time is winning the tournament.

> —JAN STEPHENSON, winner of 16 LPGA events

I didn't have to deal with that kind of subjectivity (e.g. Baseball Hall of Fame balloting). I was Pat Bradley, Hall-of-Famer, the moment I won my thirtieth.

> —PAT BRADLEY, who played her way into the LPGA Hall of Fame with thirty wins, including two majors.

———•••—•——

I used to sling the old golf club quite a distance. Tony (my brother) and I used to be dreadful. We would spend twenty minutes or longer trying to retrieve a club one of us had thrown into a tree.

> —LAURA DAVIES, native of Coventry, England, and LPGA Tour player

I've always felt that I had to prove myself. I've never felt people thought that much of me, I guess. I think anyone who has a lot of given talent probably has more pressure on them. I get mad when people say I'm a waste of talent. They don't realize how hard I work.

—BETH DANIEL, eventual winner of more than thirty LPGA tournaments, in 1983, feeling the pressure on the Tour after winning the U.S. Women's Amateur in 1975 and 1977

Dad, I won. I really played well today. Happy father's day!

—NANCY LOPEZ, calling home after winning a record fifth straight LPGA event in 1978, her rookie year

One player asked me, "Who's Mickey Wright?" I felt like slapping her.

> —KATHY POSTELWAIT, in 1993, at Mickey Wright's first tournament in eight years, the Spring Senior Challenge

---

Everyone has a dream. Mine was America, where everything seems to be number one. In Japan, I started to be a superstar, but I didn't want to be famous. Back home no star has privacy. If you have a hole in your jeans, everyone wants to know why. Here in America, nobody cares.

> —AYAKO OKOMOTO, on why she joined the LPGA Tour

All I was thinking was that I didn't have anything to wear the next day. I thought I was going to have to do laundry that night, especially after Helen [Alfredsson] hit her shot at 18. She nearly flew it into the hole.

—LAURIE MERTEN, 1993 U.S. Women's Open champion, recalling her thoughts in the final round, anticipating a playoff

———

They thought I was somebody just walking, hanging out in the rough.

—HELEN ALFREDSSON, contender in the 1994 U.S. Women's Open, commenting on how a marshal mistook her for a spectator

I had a strange feeling. I do remember walking down the 15th fairway, which has always been something of a turning point in the event [the Nabisco Dinah Shore]. I had a weird sensation that it was my tournament to win. It was strange, because under normal circumstances you feel like throwing up.

—DOTTIE MOCHRIE, on winning the 1992 Nabisco Dinah Shore, and LPGA major

It's nice to be well liked, but it's even better to be well liked and respected.

—MEG MALLON, winner of the 1991 U.S. Women's Open, after being named the LPGA's "Most Popular Player" in 1990

The zone is a funny area. You can't explain when people look at you, they can see it, though. What you see, well, it's more like what you don't see. You don't see anything but a four-inch-wide strip right in front of your face. Everything else disappears. The tents are gone, the people are gone, everything is gone. And it takes a while to get out of it.

—PATTY SHEEHAN, member of the LPGA Hall of Fame, on being focused on the golf course

I opened the door in my hotel and I was trying to get my newspaper. I didn't have any clothes on and I figured it was safe because it was 5:45 in the morning. I open it up and there is this guy there going, "Hope you win your thirtieth soon." I looked at the guy and said, "Thanks. How did you know it was me?" He said, "Oh, I'd recognize you anywhere."

—AMY ALCOTT, seeking her thirtieth LPGA win in 1994 to become eligible for the Hall of Fame

When I finally quit, for the first time in my life I am going to unpack everything, get all of my clothes pressed, and put them on hangers. I used to love the Tour when I first started because I didn't have to make my own bed. Now I hate living in motels. I want to come home.

—NANCY LOPEZ, in 1984, after having her first child

We'll either hire someone to travel with me or my mom will do it. Just because you've had a baby doesn't mean you can't win tournaments. Nancy Lopez proved that.

—JULIE INKSTER, in 1989, explaining how she will handle competitive golf and motherhood

Adeline was looking up at him tenderly. "May I come, too, and walk round with you?" Cuthbert's bosom heaved, "Oh," he said, with a tremor in his voice, "that you would walk round with me for life!"

—P. G. WODEHOUSE, *The Clicking of Cuthbert* (1922)

All you had to do was look at her. She has all the ability in the world. She can drive, chip, putt. All her shots are top class. And her temperament. She's an ice-cool Swede, one of the best talents in the world.

—LAURA DAVIES, assessing Anika Sorenstam's talent

Turning pro is something I've wanted to do ever since I was twelve, and this is the time to go for it. I gave this a great deal of thought, talked a lot about it with my parents, and there was never a question in my mind. Tiger Woods did it. He's out there, and that was an inspiration to me. There are no more set standards in golf. You don't have to be twenty-five to turn pro. You just have to feel like I do, have a burning inside for the game.

> —CHRISTIE KERR, at age nineteen, explaining why she turned down a scholarship to Stanford to join the LPGA Tour

It's definitely been a learning experience, not just in golf but in general. The biggest adjustment has been not knowing where I'm going, how I'm going to get there . . . and when I get to a new town it seems as though I get lost every time.

—VICKI GOETZE, winner of the 1989 and 1992 U.S. Women's Amateur and the 1992 NCAA Championship, adjusting to the Tour

I'm coming home and I'm bringing home the trophy and it's a big one.

—JULIE INKSTER, to her daughters, after winning the 1999 U.S. Women's Open

11

Caddies

. . . The professional of their boyhood's days had been in many ways a good fellow enough, but his chances had been comparatively few and his temptations many. There were very few greens (clubs) that needed or could afford a professional and so, unless he was one of the few lucky and resolute ones he never rose far above the status of the caddie from which he originally emerged, and when hard times or old age overtook him, he ended as he had begun.

—BERNARD DARWIN, from *The Darwin Sketchbook*

A day of clubs, a silver town or two,
A flask of scotch, a pipe of shag—and thou
Beside me caddying in the wilderness—
Ah, wilderness were paradise enow

—H. W. BOYNTON in *The Golfer's Rubaiyat*

The player may experiment about with his swing, his grip, his stance. It is only when he begins asking his caddies' advice that he is getting on dangerous ground.

—SIR WALTER SIMPSON, in his book *The Art of Golf* (1887)

The professional [caddie] is a reckless, feckless creature. In the golfing season in Scotland he makes money all the day and spends it all the night. His sole loves are golf and whiskey.

—HORACE HUTCHINSON, golf writer and golfer, in 1900

. . . It is not impossible that the caddie knows less about the game than yourself, and, on the other hand, his views as to the best thing to do in a particular situation are often regulated by what he has seen the scratch men do at such times. You may not be a scratch man.

—HARRY VARDON, in his book *Some General Hints*

One time the caddies talked of a strike unless wages were raised. Ross heard of this, walked to the caddie pen, and asked the leader what was going on. Hearing the grievance, he whacked the caddie on the head with his everpresent five-iron and informed him the strike was over.

> —ROD INNES, remembering noted golf architect Donald Ross at early 20th century Pinehurst, in the book *Pinehurst Stories* (1991) by Lee Pace

There are three things in the world that he held in the smallest esteem—slugs, poets and caddies with hiccups.

> —P. G. WODEHOUSE in "Rodney Fails to Qualify" (1924)

Remember the basic rule: Make friends with your caddie and the game will make friends with you. How true this is. It is easy to arrange that your guest opponent shall be deceived into undertipping his caddie at the end of the morning round, so that the news gets round among the club employees that your opponent is a no good, and the boys will gang up against him.

—STEPHEN POTTER, in his article "Golfsmanship," in *The Atlantic Monthly* (1948)

Look here, sir. I'll give you the club, you play the bloody shot.

—WILLIE BLACK, Muirfield caddie, to Bobby Cruickshank in 1925

It'll take three good ones to be on in two t'day sir.

> —A CADDIE to Henry Longhurst, playing into a stiff wind

You know Deane Beman? When he han' the money out, he look at you like you done stab him in the knee.

> —A CADDIE's remarks in George Plimpton's essay "They Also Serve"

Why ask me? You've asked me two times already and paid no attention to what I said. Pick your own club.

> —DOW FINSTERWALD'S CADDIE, in the 1960 U.S. Open

I knew nothing about caddying at first, but it wasn't difficult to learn. The other caddies, though, didn't like to see any new ones, because that might mean they wouldn't get a job sometime. So they had what they called a "kangaroo court." It was like a fraternity initiation. They'd form two lines and we'd have to run between them while each one of them gave us a good hard lick with their belts as we ran by. Sometimes they'd get a barrel and put a new kid in it and roll it down this big hill that the clubhouse sat atop of. That was worse than running the gauntlet, but for some reason, they never did that to me.

—BYRON NELSON, remembering his caddying days in Texas, in *How I Played The Game* (1993)

I'm doin' the playin' and my caddie's chokin'.

—LEE TREVINO, when he couldn't find his caddie at the 1971 U.S. Open at Merion

Little brother, I don't do traps and I don't go into the weeds.

—A CADDIE, to PGA professional Fuzzy Zoeller

Very few caddies make good tees. The ball should be just perched on the sand so that none of the latter can be seen. . . .

—HARRY VARDON, in *How to Play Golf* (ca. 1912, in the days before manufactured tees)

It was one of the greatest thrills of my life. I remember she was wearing tennis shoes and outdistancing the other ladies by twenty yards.

—PAUL AZINGER, recalling the time he caddied for Mickey Wright

I know you can be fined for throwing a club, but I want to know if you can get fined for throwing a caddie?

—TOMMY BOLT, winner of 11 PGA Tour events

If a permanent caddie is heroin, if you're going to break out in a cold sweat because you don't have him, then you'd better get one.

—FRANK BEARD, U.S. Senior Tour player

. . . better tournament golf scoring was particularly due to the Depression because it induced thousands of urchins who might otherwise have been playing baseball or annoying their parents to earn an honest dollar by caddying.

—NOEL F. BUSH, in *The New Yorker* in 1937

How much money do I have? If I knew I wouldn't have very much, would I?

> —JOE JEMSEK, former Depression-era caddie who became owner of Cog Hill and other fine golf courses in the Chicago area

It is a game of tradition, one we'd like to maintain. Plus, I don't think their long legs look very good.

> —REG MURPHY, USGA President, explaining why he declined to allow caddies to wear shorts during the searing heat of the 1994 U.S. Open at Oakmont

All you've got is your bag carriers now. All they can do is give the golfer a weather report—not the right club.

—ALFIE, Tom Watson's caddie, at the 1977 British Open at Turnberry

Shots like that are a little too much for a 24-year-old heart, Dad.

—CADDIE JACKIE NICKLAUS to his father Jack, after he almost put his tee shot into Rae's Creek on the par-d thirteenth during the final round of the 1986 Masters

12

Competition

... and again Paradise played its part, this time a less heavenly one, because he robbed me of a hole by playing what I still think is one of the best shots I ever saw, with a wooden club off a wet road, right over the woods and on to the green. However, I won the match by a hole, and the air was full of trumpets and rose-colored clouds.

> —BERNARD DARWIN, on defeating Horace Hutchinson in match play in 1900

I play golf with friends but we don't play friendly golf.

—BEN HOGAN

———◆✦◆———

When making a match, do not try to get a greater allowance of strokes than that to which you are entitled on your handicap, alleging to your opponent that the said handicap is an unfair one. Your opponent may think you are a little too "keen"; and if he grants your improper request, and you should win the match, he may think some other things besides.

—HARRY VARDON from *Some General Hints*

What is love compared with holing out before your opponent?

—P. G. WODEHOUSE

He smiles as he plays, but it is not a broad smile, just a faint flicker over his features. It is what you might call the Vardonic Smile. He was never a worrier, or recounter of lost strokes. Nothing ruffled him. He sank into the game but there was nothing grim about him. No teeth grinding or setting of jaw.

—ANDREW KIRKALDY, British golf professional, recalling Harry Vardon

My dad always told me, "Don't lift weights, you will lose your feel and your touch." David and Tiger have proven that you can keep your swing and keep your touch, and they are better, stronger golfers for it.

—DAVIS LOVE III, commenting on the conditioning programs of PGA Tour rivals Tiger Woods and David Duval in 2000

I've heard players speak proudly of fifth-place finishes. If you can be happy with fifth, it could be that you don't have what it takes to win.

—MICKEY WRIGHT, winner of 82 LPGA events, commenting on the LPGA Tour in 1976

I know how to choke. Given even a splinter-thin opportunity to let my side down and destroy my own score, I will seize it. Not only does ice water not run through my veins, but what runs there has a boiling point lower than body temperature.

—JOHN UPDIKE, in *Golf Digest* in 1995

I'm a guy who'll play with amateurs. A $50 Nassau, $500, $5,000 or nothing. It doesn't matter. I just like to play.

—LEE TREVINO, in *Golf Digest* in 1994

We had breakfast together the morning of the final, drove to the course in the same car, and though the match was equally important to each of us, there was no feeling of enmity. Helen played the better golf during the morning round, and I was two holes behind when it ended. The afternoon round started, and I happened to have a streak of the best golf I have ever played in my life. On the last nine holes we played, Helen took 36 strokes and I took 32. The match ended in a 4 and 3 victory for me. The entire match had been a battle of golf shots—a pleasure to play and, unless a great many people were being untruthful, a pleasure to watch.

—VIRGINIA VAN WIE, describing a 1934 match play win over Helen Hicks

My girls were getting close to college age. And that was the main reason I did it. They needed some more money for school.

—ALLEN DOYLE, in 1999, on why he joined the Senior Tour

I think professional golfers are the most competitive athletes of all. Every time out, we play against the whole league. The league never has a bad day either.

—JIM COLBERT, winner of 8 PGA Tour events and over $3 million on the Senior Tour

I have not played golf with anyone, man or woman, amateur or professional, who made me feel so utterly outclassed.

—BOBBY JONES, commenting on Joyce Wethered

———•••••———

If you ever see a man who has tied with another for a medal, toying in the luncheon interval with a bisquit and a lemon soda, you may go out and bet your modest half-crown against that man with a light heart. But if you see him doctoring himself with a beefsteak and a bottle of beer, or better still, a pint of champagne, you may go forth and back that man with as stout a heart as though you had partaken of his luncheon.

—HORACE HUTCHINSON, in *Hints on Match and Medal Play* (1890)

He didn't beat me, sir. I beat myself, I beat myself.

—J. H. TAYLOR, winner of five British Opens (1894–5, 1900, 1909, 1913), after losing a match

Never bet with anyone you meet on the first tee who has a deep suntan, a one-iron in his bag, and squinty eyes.

—DAVE MARR, winner of the 1965 PGA Championship

The lord hates a coward.

—BYRON NELSON, to himself during his 1937 Masters win

Who the hell was that?

—BEN HOGAN, reacting to a skied 100-yard drive by
Bob Toski

Roberto, the clubs got heavy.

—LEE TREVINO, to Robert De Vicenzo after losing a lead
on the last two holes of a tournament

Why don't you come down here and play me! Come on, come on. You and your kid too. I'll give you two a side and play your low ball.

—TOMMY BOLT, conversing with God, after missing a
short putt

To anyone else, perhaps the fact that I had beaten Cecil Leitch was unimportant—an off-day for the champion. To me it was the beginning of a successful career. I had gained confidence I needed so badly. My nerves became steadier, my shot bolder. No opponent held any terror for me.

—GLENNA COLLETT, after defeating Cecil Leitch 1-up in the Berthelly Cup Matches at the Huntington Valley Country Club near Philadelphia in 1921

The one thing that Hogan and Snead and I had in common was that we wanted to beat somebody.

—BYRON NELSON

There must be nothing in sport quite like a golf match involving girls. Take the fourth-round contest between Miss Conley and Miss Sue Lance, another sixteen-year-old, from Woodland, California. When they reached the eighth green, Miss Lance lagged her approach putt to within two feet of the hole. She looked at her opponent, who was standing motionless at the side of the green. "Aren't you going to give me that putt?", Miss Lance asked. Miss Conley turned on her very best map-of-Erin smile, shook her head and replied, "I know how you putt Susan." Thereupon Miss Lance, with a great show of disdain, walked up to her ball and rapped it in backhand. The opponents walked to the next tee giggling.

—FRANK HANNIGAN, golf journalist, reporting on the 1963 U.S. Women's Amateur

Hey, I won three times and I never even got an outhouse.

> —JIMMY DEMARET, the first three-time Masters winner, commenting on bridges built to honor Gene Sarazen and Byron Nelson at Augusta National

Before I hit that shot I remember standing there thinking that all I needed to win was a 4, just to get it up there on the green and then down in two putts. That's where I made my mistake, thinking about something besides the ball. If I'd just kept my mind on swinging the club properly there wouldn't have been any problem.

> —ARNOLD PALMER'S account of his double-bogey six on the 72nd hole, costing him the 1962 Masters by one stroke

Give me a man with a fast backswing and a fat wallet.

—GOLF HUSTLER'S ANCIENT SLOGAN

. . . I have another reason for saying you should always play hard to win, apart from the fact that it improves your golf. I think you owe it to your opponent. For my own part I should feel insulted if I found out that my opponent had purposefully eased up because he felt sorry for me. . . . Anyway, a man who cannot take a thrashing in good part is usually intolerable when he is doing the thrashing.

—GARY PLAYER, in *Play Golf with Gary Player*

Then came the playoff. This was one of the rare occasions when I was so keyed up my stomach was upset, even during the night. I lost my breakfast the next morning, which I thought might be a good sign because I had always played well when I became that sick beforehand.

—BYRON NELSON, before his 18-hole playoff win, 69–70, against Ben Hogan in the 1942 Masters

I guess I must have choked.

—BERT YANCEY, after a final round score of 76 cost him the 1968 U.S. Open championship

... [Great players] learn that they don't need to play their best golf to win. They only need to shoot the lowest score.

—RICK REILLY, sports writer, in his essay "Bank Shot"

I key myself to when I'm in contention coming down to those last few holes. It is a miserable, sick, lonely feeling. You're so scared, sometimes you can't see. But when I can pull off a good shot on those holes, that's what I look forward to. And I figure I haven't won nearly enough.

—SANDRA PALMER, winner of 21 LPGA events

When their names are mentioned, which is all too infrequently, there is almost invariably a shade of sadness that accompanies names of men who are remembered not as winners but as losers.

—HERBERT WARREN WIND, commenting on Macdonald Smith, Leo Diegel and Harry Copper, excellent shotmakers, golfer's golfers, who never won a national championship

Forget it. I can beat any two players in this tournament by myself. If I need any help, I'll let you know.

—BABE ZAHARIAS, reassuring her partner Peggy Kirk Bell, who was nervous at the start of a four-ball event

Qualifying competitions are dull things unless they are cruel.

—BERNARD DARWIN, British golf journalist and member of Britain's first Walker Cup team in 1922

When I used to gamble, I looked for players with head covers on their irons. Those guys I could beat.

—CHI-CHI RODRIGUEZ, winner of 8 PGA Tour events and more than $5 million on the Senior Tour

---

I'm terrible! No one could be two up on the 16th and lose.

—LAURA BAUGH, to her father, after losing out to Hollis Stacey in the 1971 U.S. Girls' Junior

13

Architecture

Rough open ground; especially, a tract of low-lying seaside land on the east coast of the lowlands held by a town as a common and used from the Middle Ages onward for sports, including archery, bowls, and golf. Such land is characteristically sandy, tree-less, undulating or hummocky, often with dunes and the typical ground cover is bent grass with gorse bushes.

—Peter Davies, describing the nature of early Scottish linksland golf courses, "designed by God" in his reference *The Historical Dictionary of Golf* (1992)

Gorse, a low brambly shrub of the genus *ulex,* is common to Scottish wastelands and golfing links. It is said by some to grow as well in the fields of hell.

> —MICHAEL MURPHY, in his book *Golf in the Kingdom* (1972)

The example of public-spirited park commissioners of New York . . . in providing public links in Van Cortlandt Park, is bearing good fruit.

> —C. TURNER, from an article in *The Outing* in 1896 praising the opening of the first municipal public golf course in the United States

Broadly speaking, the penal school follows more or less the methods of Tom Morris and the brothers Dunn, in scattering plenty of bunkers in places most likely to catch inaccurate shots.

—TOM SIMPSON, golf course architect, in his book *The Game of Golf* (1931)

Broadly speaking, the penal school follows more or less the methods of Tom Morris and the brothers Dunn, in scattering plenty of bunkers in places most likely to catch inaccurate shots.

This is the essence of strategic architecture: to encourage initiative, reward a well-played stroke, and yet to insist that there must be planning and honest self-appraisal behind the daring.

—ROBERT TRENT JONES, SR., designer of over 400 golf courses, on strategic design in 1954

The object of inventors is to reduce the skill required for golf. If it were not for the counterskill of architects, the game would be emasculated.

> —JOHN L. LOW, a founder of the Oxford and Cambridge golfing society in 1897

———

Gentlemen, the defense rests. I think the hole is eminently fair.

> —ROBERT TRENT JONES, SR., in 1954, responding to criticism of a par-3 hole at Baltusrol that he redesigned for the U.S. Open, after scoring an ace on the hole to illustrate his point

Saw a course you'd really like, Trent. On the first tee you drop the ball over your left shoulder.

—JIMMY DEMARET, to Robert Trent Jones, Sr., designer of Spyglass Hill, Mauna Kea, Firestone, and many other courses

———•◦•◦•———

Wind and rain are great challenges. They separate the real golfers. Let the seas pound against the shore, let the rain pour.

—TOM WATSON, winner of 8 majors and 32 PGA Tour events

To this day Taylor has extremely strong views about that bunker, and he has been heard to suggest that its creator should be buried in it with a niblick through his heart . . .

> —BERNARD DARWIN, on J. H. Taylor's reaction to the fourth hole at Prestwick where took a seven in the 1914 British Open

---

Before I got out of the rough in one tournament it had turned into a shopping center.

> —BOB HOPE, on his poor play in a pro-am tournament

I fell violently in love with Cypress Point. But I was so furious because I was so besotted with the beauty of it that I just couldn't hit a golf ball.

—ENID WILSON, member of the first British Curtis Cup team (1932), on visiting Cypress Point in 1931

REPORTER: What does it (Hazeltine) lack?

HILL: Eighty acres of corn and a few cows. They ruined a good farm when they built this course.

—DAVE HILL'S critique of Hazeltine after the second round of the 1970 U.S. Open

Ninety-seven percent of the field, myself included, are not equipped to play this course. We just don't have the shots. I heard Byron Nelson say on television that 272 would win here. I couldn't shoot 272 if I got a mulligan on every hole.

—GEORGE ARCHER, commenting on Merion before the 1971 U.S. Open. Nicklaus and Trevino tied in regulation at 280 and Trevino shot a 68 to win the playoff by three shots. Archer shot 283.

I vowed that I would bring this monster to its knees.

—BEN HOGAN, commenting on Oakland Hills after he successfully defended his U.S. Open title there in 1951

Hell, man, Ray Charles could play here . . . and it still wouldn't make no difference.

—LEE TREVINO, discussing the subtleties of Muirfield during the 1972 British Open

Pine Valley is an examination in golf.

—BERNARD DARWIN'S appraisal of one of the world's best and most difficult tests of golf

Foursomes have left the first tee there and have never been seen again. They just find their shoelaces and bags.

—BOB HOPE, evaluating Pine Valley

———•••———

I've never seen Augusta so beautiful. If heaven is this pretty, I'd go there tomorrow.

—GENE SARAZEN, winner of the 1935 Masters, in 1981

The basic principles of what constitutes a great golf course are:

1. A really great course must be pleasurable to the greatest possible number.
2. It must require strategy as well as skill or it cannot be enduringly interesting.
3. It must give the average player a fair chance and at the same time require the utmost from the expert who tries for subpar scores.
4. All natural beauty should be preserved, natural hazards utilized and a minimus of artificiality introduced.

> —The principles ALISTER MACKENZIE and BOBBY JONES agreed to before designing Augusta National

I stood at the top of the hill before that fine old house and looked at the wide stretch of land rolling down the slope before me. It was cleared land for the most part, and you could take in the whole vista all the way down to Rae's Creek. I knew instantly it was the kind of terrain I had always hoped to find. I had been told, of course, about the marvelous trees and plants, but I was still unprepared for the great bonus of beauty Fruitlands offered. Frankly, I was overwhelmed by the exciting possibilities of a golf course set in the midst of such a nursery.

—BOBBY JONES, viewing the 365-acre Fruitlands nursery which was transformed into Augusta National in the 1930s

Most of the courses today, the guys shoot twenty under par and think they've accomplished something. They can't do it at PGA West because you can't hit it crooked and score. Golf was meant to be a great game of skill, not just strength. You get around here you have to have some skills.

—CHI-CHI RODRIGUEZ, assessing PGA West

I've got no business going to the U.S. Open this week and playing a hard course like Medinah.

—LOU GRAHAM, before winning the 1975 U.S. Open in a playoff against John Mahaffey at Medinah

It is today an accepted principle of golfing architecture that the tiger should be teased and trapped and tested, while the rabbit should be left to peace, since he can make his own hell for himself.

—BERNARD DARWIN, on how course design affects the low handicapper (tiger) and middle to high handicappers (rabbits)

———

... this is the first time in the history of golf that a course has been designed specifically to test the best female players in the game.

—Golf architect REES JONES commenting on his recently opened LPGA International golf course in 1995

Until the days of Allan Robertson in the second quarter of the nineteenth century and his successor Old Tom Morris who lived into the twentieth, man did not change existing land to create golfing grounds. In the homeland of golf, Scots played for centuries on terrain that was entirely natural. These natural links of Scotland form the foundation of the practice of golf architecture even today.

—GEOFFREY S. CORNISH, golf architect and writer

My God, you can get starting times in six different languages.

—THOMAS P. "TIP" O'NEIL, JR., former Speaker of the U.S. House of Representatives, commenting on the Cambridge, Massachusetts course renamed in his honor after he retired from politics

———

But here, the 100-player, the 80-player, the 75-player, has only one shot to play from the sand; and neither boldness nor skill will help him correct a position which may not have been his fault in the first place. He has one shot—the blast. That is all.

—TED RAY, noting the unfairness of Oakmont's furrowed bunkers during the 1927 U.S. Open

The object of the bunker or trap, is not only to punish a physical mistake, to punish a lack of control, but also to punish pride and egotism. I believe in leaving a way open for a player who can only drive one hundred yards, if he can keep that drive straight. But the one I am after is the golfer who thinks he can carry one hundred and eighty yards when one hundred and sixty is his limit. So I believe one of the best systems of trapping or arranging bunkers is to let the player make his own choice, from either the shorter or longer route and go for that.

—CHARLES B. MACDONALD, "father of American golf architecture" and designer of The National Golf Links of America, the Chicago Golf Club and other classic venues

You gotta sneak up on these holes. Iffen you clamber and clank up on'em, they're liable to turn round and bite you.

> —SAM SNEAD, commenting on Oakmont, one of golf's most penal courses, during the 1953 U.S. Open

———•••••———

While I have never met Pete Dye, I know him well. He is 500 years old and has absorbed the wisdom of the ages. He has a pointed hat and a flowing robe embroidered with occult symbols. When he speaks, he becomes extremely animated, and gesticulates a lot with flashes of blue static crackling from his long fingernails.

> —PETER DOBEREINER, on golf course builder Pete Dye, whose courses are sometimes considered diabolical

Apparently a nephew of Macdonald's wasn't all that impressed with the par-4 first hole and bragged to his uncle that he could drive the green. Macdonald told him that was impossible, but the nephew continued to boast. Soon the two men ascended the first tee, whereupon the nephew hit a perfect tee shot that cleared all the bunkers at the seam of the dogleg, bounced on the fairway, then leaped up on the green. The nephew stood by proudly, awaiting his laudations, only to have Macdonald stomp from the tee into his house, where legend has it he promptly struck the name of his nephew from his will.

—PETE DYE, relating a story about Charles B. Macdonald and the National Golf Links in his book *Bury Me in a Pot Bunker* (1995)

Where are the windmills and animals?

—Fuzzy Zoeller, commenting on Pete Dye's TPC
Stadium Course at Sawgrass

———

Don't give me the excuse that you weren't standing
there, and you approved it. I don't want to listen to
your alibis, let's just fix the hole.

—Alice Dye, amateur golf champion and the first
woman to become a member of the American Society of
Golf Course Architects, to her husband Pete, on a golf
course construction site

When I do a course that is in the trees and hills, it has to evolve. But any time we get a flat piece of property, I'll just take a piece of paper and sketch it. I never even saw the site at Grand Cypress before construction. What is there to see on Central Florida flat ground. I mean, the only time you go is really just to pacify the owner.

> —JACK NICKLAUS, designer of Grand Cypress and many other golf courses, in 1991

———

I'm not going back to a place where they never rake the goddamn bunkers.

> —BEN HOGAN, after winning the 1953 British Open at Carnoustie

Make no mistake, here is greatness and mystery that strange element which is both real magic, sleight of hand, and a brilliant just keeping "the windy side of the law" . . . In that same way as Jupiter would descend as a swan or a bull or a shower of golf to gratify desire . . . or Proteus in wrestling changed shape and form most alarmingly, so St. Andrews will employ every means to deceive, flatter, cajole or dragoon you into loving it, and into admitting its mastery of you. Now, nobody who plays once or twice, or twenty or thirty times will begin to know this links at all. That takes years or a lifetime.

—PATRIC DICKINSON, in his book *A Round of Golf Courses: A Selection of the Best Eighteen* (1951)

14

Abroad

The older inhabitants of St. Andrews may be indifferent to catastrophes, but all of them are golfers bound together in one common enthusiasm for the game. It is talked of, thought of, practiced by all. When I have stayed there, even in the shops, I have found the same lively interest. The chemist hopes I am finding the course to my liking, the stationer asks me how I am playing; and the hairdresser, to whom I have paid a hurried visit, is plainly more interested in my golf than my coiffure.

—JOYCE WETHERED, English lady golf champion on what it was like to be in Andrews in the 1920s and 1930s

Gentlemen, this beats rifle shooting. It is a game I think might go in our country.

> —American WILLIAM K. VANDERBILT in Biarritz at the end of the nineteenth century, when he saw Willie Dunn, the famous golf architect and professional hit a few practice shots

Think of teeing off in the land where bairns cut their teeth on niblicks and brassies, and the nineteenth hole still thrives—bonny Scotland, the gowfer's paradise.

> —AN AD IN *GOLF ILLUSTRATED* for the White Star Line in 1929

The simple truth is I love Scottish golf and all the peculiar experience that embraces—the puny flag-sticks that make a hole look 150 yards longer than it really is, the warm ale, a noname links with simple honor boxes, the clubhouse toilets that seem to have no flush handle, and the caddies that squint over a pinched cigarette and seem to advise "Best to shoot for the church spires yonder, mate. The Presbyterian one, of course."

—JAMES DODSON, in his essay "Golf in the Homeland" (1997)

... on the last two rounds each of the girls went out in a foursome made up of three club members partnered with her in a best-ball event, the members using their respective handicaps and the lady pros playing at scratch. A playing arrangement like the one that obtained in Havana puts more of a burden on the player, the pro, than may appear at first glance. Patty Berg, for example, drew as her partners: 1. A dashing young air force major who serves as President Batista's personal pilot; 2. A delicate middle-aged señora who wore a colossal visor that shielded her entire face from the sun—a bronzed complexion is less highly prized in Cuban society than ours; 3. A peppy, sociable little fellow who was in the throes of that international virus, the slice.

—FROM A *SPORTS ILLUSTRATED* article, "The Big Three,"
regarding Patty Berg, Betty Jameson and Louise Suggs,
all members of the LPGA Hall of Fame, in Cuba in 1956

One interesting thing happened during one of those exhibitions—a plague of locusts. The air was so thick with them that every time you swung the club you'd kill six or seven of them and have to wipe off the club before you could hit again. Kind of upset your stomach, really. You could hardly see for all the locusts in the air, plus you'd crunch dozens of them under your feet when you walked. We played three holes before they finally called a halt.

> —BYRON NELSON, describing a 1937 exhibition tour in Argentina

Sorry, I don't play golf while on vacation.

> —BEN HOGAN, when asked if he was available to play a round of golf with the King of Belgium

What else is there to do over there? Wear a skirt?

—GEORGE LOW, on his need to play golf in his father's
native Scotland

A reasonable number of fleas is good for a dog. It
keeps the dog forgetting that he is a dog.

—WALTER TRAVIS, to friends in reaction to real and
imagined slights from the British, prior to the 1904
British Amateur which Travis won at Sandwich

I'm tired of giving it my best and not having it be good enough.

> —JACK NICKLAUS, after losing the British Open by one shot at Turnberry in 1977

———

One of the prerequisites to win a major championship is to enter the damn thing. You are not going to win the British Open by correspondence.

> —TOM KITE, criticizing exempt U.S. players who fail to play in the British Open

You stop this nonsense or I'll take the Royal out of St. George's.

> —THE PRINCE OF WALES, admonishing a steward in the St. George's clubhouse who claimed he could not serve Walter Hagen and Gene Sarazen, the Prince's guests

———

Wee wheels in ya head sir. You've got to forget those bloody wee wheels sir.

> —SANDY MATHESON, a caddie at Dornoch, to writer Rick Reilly

It is a pity you will not be following in the footsteps of Francis Ouimet and Robert Tyre Jones. But it is splendid that you should be following in the footsteps of Lafayette and Churchill. However, a senior member asks me to remind you that we are twenty years more ancient than the First Continental Congress, and maybe you should get your priorities straight.

> —KEITH MACKENZIE, from the Royal & Ancient Golf Club of St. Andrews, Scotland, lightly admonishing Alistair Cooke, who addressed the U.S. House of Representatives on the bicentennial of the First Continental Congress in 1974, thus having to cancel his appointment to speak at the St. Andrews Annual Dinner

I hope they regret it the rest of their lives.

> —INTERNATIONAL TEAM CAPTAIN DAVID GRAHAM on the
> players who elected not to compete in the inaugural
> President's Cup in 1994

They interested us immensely by bringing with them huge quantities of clubs and balls—the latter for practice purposes—which were carted about the countryside in the most awe-inspiring voluminous leather caddie bags.

> —ENID WILSON, describing the American team's
> preparation for an informal match against the British in
> 1930. This event foreshadowed the Curtis Cup matches,
> which began in 1932.

What a joy it is to jump into the train in the evening at a London terminus, with one's clubs on the rack overhead, and to wake the next morning to the sounds of Edinburgh and then the strange hum of the train rumbling over Firth Bridge. A few battle-ships lie quiet and still far beneath, dull shapes in the hazy morning light which is slowly uncovering the stretches of the Firth and the little groups of houses clustered along the shore.

It is a journey as full of charm and interest as the destination we are bound for. The last mile or so runs down the side of the links and the first exciting glimpse of St. Andrews is caught. All too soon the train carries us ahead, wreathing the seventeenth tee in its smoke as it chugs into the gloom of the station.

—JOYCE WETHERED, in her essay "The Essence of Scottish Golf" in 1933

While PGA touring professionals have been brought up on manicured courses since junior golf, the foreign contingent have been raised on bad lies and rough weather requiring mental toughness.

> —Pete Dye, noting why international golfers have reached parity with or have surpassed the Americans

We learned to play foursomes from the Americans. For years, every time we had a shot to play, we would always confer with our partner. It was sort of a cop-out, really, sharing the responsibility. The Americans never did that. Each played her own game and took responsibility for the shot.

> —John Bailey, husband of Diane Bailey, captain of the 1986 Curtis Cup team

The Americans respect you more as a player. Australians don't appreciate their own players. They feel like you are a traitor to leave the country and do well. I think they are jealous. Maybe it stems from the war. Maybe people think the Americans came over, met the prettiest girls and took them back to America.

—Jan Stephenson, LPGA professional and native of Australia in 1991

When Jack Nicklaus told me I was playing Seve Ballesteros, I took so many pills that I'm glad they don't have drug tests for golfers.

—Fuzzy Zoeller, on his 1983 Ryder Cup match which he halved

. . . allowance must always be made for the strange-
ness of a strange land. When Bobby Jones first played
our championship [British Open] he tore up his card
and drove the ball out to sea; when Hagen first
played he finished something like fiftieth place. It is
hard work to play a game in the other fellow's country, and it seems that a probationary visit is needed
before even the greatest can give of their best.

—BERNARD DARWIN, in his classic *The Darwin Sketch Book*

You don't expect to be hit by a small white ball while walking through a meadow in Russia.

> —PROFESSOR ALEXY NIKOLOV, before Perestroika, noting that fewer than 300 Russians play golf

Did you know? You have to demonstrate a minimum competence just to get on the course. You need a "green card."

> —Sweden's JESPER PARNEVIK, 1994 British Open runnerup, describing the protocol of Swedish golf

The other factor (in addition to the turf) that unbuttons us on linkslands, in my view, is the bunkers. Never call a Scottish bunker a sand trap, at least not in the presence of your Scottish host. . . . They are designed to penalize you for making a stupid shot rather than frame a pretty green fairway or provide a soft white cushion for your 6-iron shot to the green . . ."

—JAMES DODSON, in his essay "Golf in the Homeland" (1997)

Doook! Doook! You forgot to pay your green fee!

—BESSIE FENN, manager of The Breakers Golf Operations, chasing the Duke of Windsor after he had finished the first hole

15

Media, Galleries, and Fans

. . . attending a golf tournament is like trying to watch a 144-ring circus. The game is diffused over four miles of ground where the winning and losing are worked out in no particular corner, and not in a few hours but four days.

—AL BARKOW, in his book *Golf's Golden Grind*

That wee body in the red jack canna play gouf.

—A SPECTATOR, commenting on Allan Robertson's poor play in a match where he was partnered with Tom Morris against the Dunn brothers in 1849. Robertson, the first noteworthy golf professional, was the leading player of his era.

The sonofabitch went in!

—JIMMY DEMARET, describing Lew Worsham's 140-yard eagle approach shot on the final hole which won him the 1953 World Championship of Golf

Our ship docked in New York on June 8 (1928) and the welcome was really tremendous. A wonderful band at the dock kept playing "Among my Souvenirs" and thousands of golf fans and thousands more who didn't know one club from another lined the streets. The late Mayor Jimmy Walker welcomed me at City Hall following a long motor ride down Fifth Avenue, with police on motorcycles and enthusiastic children waving and yelling to me. At the City Hall Mayor Walker presented me with the key to the City of New York.

—WALTER HAGEN, describing the reception he received after he won the 1928 British Open

Hagen was at home with all classes of society, far more than Dempsey or Ruth, the other great champions of the twenties, whom he resembled in the blackness of his hair, his amazing magnetism, his love of admiring crowds, and his rise from humble beginnings.

—GENE SARAZEN, in his book *Thirty Years of Championship Golf*

The gallery becomes almost a part of the course and part of the round, to the experienced competitor, either he can play with a gallery following him or he can't—and if he can't, of course, the gallery doesn't follow him.

—BOBBY JONES

I would have worried if he didn't want a photograph.

> —BABE ZAHARIAS, regarding an overzealous
> photographer at the British Ladies' Championship

———

I am staying in the house on Tobacco Road that Jeeter Lester moved out of.

> —Sports writer JIM MURRAY, appraising his
> accommodations while covering the Masters in
> the old days

I'm sitting there with the press, all pleased and comfortable, and when Arnie holes the thirty-footer they leave me like I got the pox.

>—KEN VENTURI, after Palmer dropped a 30-foot birdie putt on the final hole to win the 1960 Masters which Venturi thought he had won

Golfers cannot do their best playing to empty fairways any better than actors can give a fine performance to empty chairs.

>—BOB HARLOW, the PGA's first full-time tour director, in 1929

I wouldn't be here if there wasn't a golf tournament here. They're all the same—greens, tees. I'm here because there's money to be won.

—LEE TREVINO, when asked my a gallery member whether he like the Pinehurst No.2 Course, site of the 1994 Senior Open

Most difficult of all is trying to be "a good sport." You are compelled to do many things you don't give two hoots about. To go on parties when you just long to be in bed, to be nice to all sorts of people, ask all sorts of favors.

—GLENNA COLLET VARE

Please give me the chance I've been fighting for all week.

> —HAROLD "JUG" MCSPADEN, to photographers who broke his concentration on the last hole of regulation match play in the final of the 1937 PGA Championship. He missed a four-foot putt for the win then lost to Denny Shute on the first playoff hole.

At least I'm going to get a chance to meet her.

> —A FAN who, in 1978, was bloodied when hit by an errant shot by Nancy Lopez, then in her first full year on the LPGA Tour

I just love to see you guys with long hair, because you can't see. I never saw a hippie playing golf.

> —BERT YANCEY, PGA pro and former West Point cadet, addressing the press in the 1970s

You know I thought our English football (soccer) crowds were bad, but this is worse.

> —IAN WOOSNAM, to Peter Jacobsen after hearing obscenities from the U.S. Open gallery at Medinah because Jacobsen was a known Portland Trailblazer fan and the Midwestern crowd favored the Bulls

The pitiful sights of suffering parents almost imperiled the gaiety at Stoke Pages. The poor dears endured agonies of suspense, and the management wrung shaking hands in the seclusion of the shrubbery or the darkest corners of the clubhouse while a trembling momma or pappa begged to know how the darling was getting on now . . . Perhaps Ma and Pa banished themselves feeling they could not bear the spectacle of their little one missing even a littler putt.

—ELEANOR HELME, journalist and organizer of the British Ladies' Championship from 1924 to 1938, recalling the 1924 event

I think you all know pretty well how much I feel. I suppose the sun got me a little. I got a little tired, I guess I got a little emotional coming up 18.

—ARNOLD PALMER, age 64, at a press conference after his final U.S. Open at Oakmont in 1994

I really like the attention. I guess I'm sort of a ham.

—LPGA professional, 6'2" CAROL MANN, commenting on her height and the attention it brings her

If she's dumb enough to play, I'm dumb enough to let her.

—MRS. TILLIE STACEY, mother of Hollis Stacey, then the defending Girls Junior Champion (1971), when Hollis played with tendonitis in her right wrist

———

Another great trick of well-meaning friends in a gallery following your match is that of telling you how you should play your shot . . . That is the worst pest of all because they offer advice, unsolicited as it may be, in such a way that it greatly irritates you, and it is several holes before you can control yourself, during which time your opponent may have moved out in front with a short lead.

—FRANCIS OUIMET, winner of the 1913 U.S. Open and two U.S. Amateurs (1914, 1931)

Whip the gringo!

>—LEE TREVINO'S FANS, urging him on during his
>successful run at the 1968 U.S. Open at Oak Hill

You figured out who you thought you could beat
and you challenged him. And you hoped you didn't
get Leondard Dodson because he'd pay a guy to follow you around with a camera and click it on your
backswing.

>—JIMMY DEMARET, describing how pairings were arrived
>at during the San Francisco Match Play Championship
>in the 1930s

There are questions all the time, every week, whether people know me or not. It's not just annoying, it hurts. I'm not trying to make errors, to miss a shot, but it happens. Every ounce of me is out there trying to be the best. I'm out there spilling my guts. Take Atlanta this year. I finish second behind Sandra Post. When the tournament is over, a woman comes over to me—walks right up to me and says: "What's wrong with you?" What's wrong with me? I wanted to deck her right there.

—Pat Bradley, early in her LPGA Hall of Fame career

Right here Jack.

> —SIGNS held up by Arnie's Army behind water hazards and bunkers at the 1967 U.S. Open at Baltusrol

---

... the crowd behaved in the most disgraceful manner, running in before the players and completely blocking up the entrance to the hole. Considerable delay took place before the green was with some difficulty partially cleared.

> —BERNARD DARWIN, recounting a classic challenge match between Tom Morris and Willie Park, winners of seven of the first eight British Opens between them, in 1870

I learned early that whatever I got out of life, I'd have to go out and get for myself. And the physical aptitude I possessed gave me the means at the beginning. However, I had to create a paying market for that ability to play golf. Showmanship was needed and happily I possessed a flair for that, too, and I used it. In fact some fellows sort of believed I invented the kind of showmanship which, in those early days, began to put golf on a bigtime money basis.

> —WALTER HAGEN, in his autobiography *The Walter Hagen Story*

There was one fan my caddie used to worry about. He would show up with a grocery bag. He would never come up and say anything to me. My caddie always wondered what the guy had in the bag, but he was harmless. And then there was the guy who rode a bicycle from one tournament to the next. . . . I used to get some pretty crazy people showing up in white tuxedos with bouquets, saying, "Let's get married."

—JAN STEPHENSON, in an interview in *Golf Digest* in 1991

The 1922 U.S. Open was the first USGA event with an admission fee for spectators. In less than four years, thanks to the popularity of Bobby Jones and other players, those fees became the organization's chief source of income.

—*GOLF MAGAZINE*, December 1994

I don't think we've ever achieved in golf television—
and this may be presumptuous of me—the right balance between audio and video. The developments in
the video have been just sensational, and a lot of
that was pioneered by ABC. But the audio doesn't
match that, mostly because they (announcers) talk
too much.

—SANDY TATUM of the USGA

Oh, he's waiting for the grass to grow up under the
ball and give him a better lie!

—Gallery commentary, from the book *Down the Fairway*

16

Endings

After all the noise and clamor . . . after the clubs are cleaned and stacked . . . the silence which follows the last round played seems strange, bewildering, yet wonderfully peaceful. However, this silence, to me, often reverberates with the roars and the applause of the fans who followed me for so many years. I got my name in the record books and for every golf ball I hit I got to know someone . . . caddies, kings, golf fans and even a few phonies.

—WALTER HAGEN

If they don't have golf in heaven then I'm not going.

—An inscription on a pillow in Arnold Palmer's home

His biggest game is over. He putted out.

—Pastor Edwin A. Shroeder at Walter Hagen's funeral
in October of 1969

I'm just tired. It has been a long grind. There were days when I thought I would scream if I had to go to the course. It was week-in week-out for years. I tried to give my best to golf. Now I want to realize a dream. I've got my dad and mother with me and . . . Well, that's the story.

—Byron Nelson, retiring from the professional tour in
1946 at age 34

And softly by the nineteenth hole
  reclined
Make game of that which maketh game
  of thee

> —ROBERT K. RISK in "The Golfaiyet of Dufor
> Hy-yam" (1919)

Try to feel that you are looser and more decisive on the eighteenth hole than you were on the first. Fell more likely to coin the last tournament of the season than the first.

> —DR. BOB ROTELLA, sports psychologist

On the all-too-few occasions that I met Pam Barton and played with her, I was struck at once not only by her ability as a golfer but by her simplicity and charm. It is because of these qualities that she will be so greatly missed in the golfing world. Her achievements and her character so obviously fitted her to take a leading part in ladies' golf after the war when, I am sure, fresh triumphs awaited her. She will remain as a fine example to all young golfers, and we shall remember her with great affection.

—JOYCE WETHERED, on Pam Barton's death, in an RAF airplane crash, at age 26, while in the armed services during World War II

A gouty foot probably prevented him on one occasion from winning the championship, and when he grew old rheumatism attacked him venomously in the back, so that he could hardly swing at all. Yet he continued to play with enjoyment, and I always thought this a very pleasing trait in one who had formerly regarded his weaker bretheren with a rather arrogant eye.

> —BERNARD DARWIN, describing the physical demise of Mure Ferguson

Don't ever get old.

> —BEN HOGAN, in 1971, when he had to withdraw from the Houston Open after 11 holes due to pain and fatigue

I don't want to be eulogized until I'm dead.

—BEN HOGAN, declining an invitation to be the honoree
at Jack Nicklaus' Memorial tournament

We're in a blessed drainpipe and we've got to crawl
along it till we die.

—BERNARD DARWIN, in *The Darwin Sketchbook*

Soon she returned to a Galveston hospital. Once lean and leathery at 5'6" and 148 pounds, she kept losing weight as the cancer ravaged her. She died on September 27, 1956, but in her last few months, she somehow remained alive out of sheer determination . . . Before the Babe was too ill to get out of bed, she often walked in her pajamas to the little beach on the Gulf of Mexico outside the hospital. She would take a wedge and a few golf balls with her and, one by one, she would knock the balls out into the gentle surf. . . . Those were the last golf shots she ever hit.

—DAVE ANDERSON, in his article "Remembering the Babe" in *The Golf Journal* in 1981

People have said that the Babe was a little crude once in a while, but I didn't see it that in her. No, I saw a wonderful athlete and someone with a lot of class. I remember when she was suffering from cancer so badly, she'd tell everybody it wasn't so bad, we're all going to get better. She knew she didn't have a chance but she went to hospitals telling patients they were going to get better, and so was she. You think that's a lady with class? Yes, sir. She gave everybody hope.

> —PATTY BERG, a founding player on the LPGA Tour and Hall of Famer remembering Babe Zaharias

My frustration centers on not being able to play as well as I once did. I still could play regularly, but don't want to. I was out there from 1955 through 1969. That's fifteen years of motels and competitive pressure. Now I play only a handful of events. I've played six tournaments this year. Last year I played only two.

—MICKEY WRIGHT, in a *Golf Digest* interview in 1976

I never heard a word said against him except him except a solitary complaint that, in the lightness of his heart, he played pibrochs (musical pieces on a bagpipe) round the drowsy town at the midnight hour. What would we not give to hear those pipes again.

—ANDREW LANG, remembering Scottish golfer
F. M. Tait, British Amateur champion (1896, 1898) and British Open champion (1896, 1897), who died at age 30 in the Boer War

I'm going to die in a tournament on the golf course. They'll just throw me in a bunker and build it up a little bit.

> —LEE TREVINO, winner of five Vardon Trophies for low scoring average on the PGA Tour

People have always said, "Jack, I wish I could play like you." Well now they can.

> —JACK NICKLAUS, in 1994 at age 54 and struggling with his game

I don't want to get old, but I don't have much choice, so if it will help my golf like these guys, then it won't be so bad.

—JOSE MARIA OLAZABAL, after losing to Greg Norman and Nick Price in the 1994 Grand Slam of Golf

I'm old enough to be most of their fathers. They don't know whether to call me Mr. Sigel or to call me Jay.

—JAY SIGEL, age 49, playing in his 27th consecutive U.S. Amateur in 1993 against a field dominated by college-age players

The road's getting' shorter and narrower, but I'll play wherever the pigeons land.

—SAM SNEAD, at 81 years old in early 1994

Life is a journey and it must be enjoyed—and, like golf, part of the fun is that you never know where it might take you.

—DR. BOB ROTELLA, sports psychologist

When you die, what you take with you is what you leave behind. If you don't share, no matter how much you have, you will always be poor.

> —CHI-CHI RODRIGUEZ, winner of many awards for his community service to junior golfers and others

---

Captain in 1865, Sir John (Low) played well into his 90s, and took to his pony when walking became difficult during the latter part of the round, dismounting between shots.

> —RICHARD MACKENZIE, in his book *A Wee Nip at the 19th Hole* (1991)

Julius Boros died on a golf course one quiet May afternoon and took the swing of our dreams with him. . . . No one ever swung a club with such nonchalance as Boros. He had, more than any other player of his time, the game's most exclusive quality: effortless power. And it came to him as naturally as taking a drag on a cigarette.

—JERRY TARDE, editor of *Golf Digest* in 1994

Show respect to Sarah
You golfers passing by;
She's the only person on this course,
Who can't improve her lie.

—Rhyme resulting from a golf course being built around the grave of Sarah Wallace (d. 1862) at Shore Acres

. . . For the retired warrior there are no anxieties, no agonies, no thwarted ambitions, no wretched little jealousies, no bitter regrets. Never again will he toss and tumble, thinking of the match that is before him on the morrow. No black dances of a missed putt from the march that is past will crouch beside his pillow to arouse him at midnight. He will not watch his conqueror going on daily from round to round and murmur to himself that that is where he ought to be. There will be no penitence for having been cross, for as far as the game is concerned he need never be cross any more; no miserable pretense of being a loser for there is nothing to lose.

—BERNARD DARWIN, in *The Darwin Sketchbook*

Deeply regretted by numerous friends and all golfers, he thrice in succession won the championship belt and held it without rivalry and yet without envy, his many amiable qualities being no less acknowledged than his golfing achievements.

> —The inscription on the grave of Young Tom Morris, winner of four British Opens, and the dominant player of his era, in St. Andrews

I've known you longer than anyone in golf. I can only tell you there is no help. I can only get worse, but you are not to keep thinking of it. You know that in golf we play the ball as it lies. Now, we will not speak of this again, ever.

> —BOBBY JONES'S response to writer Al Laney who was distraught over Jones's affliction with a crippling disease in the late 1940s. Jones was confined to a wheel chair until his death in 1971 at the age of 69.

Index